About the Author

Robert Purse has over 40 years of experience in the management of people, experience that has been gained in a wide range of sectors (both private and public). He has worked in organisations ranging from micro-businesses to multi-nationals, from software development to airports. In his spare time, he enjoys gardening and keeping koi. He plays the Irish harp badly, but enthusiastically.

Dedication

This book is dedicated to my grandson, Alfie Claude Gerrard-Purse, and to my parents, 'Nel' and Arthur Purse.

Robert Purse

THE MANAGEMENT OF PEOPLE

AUSTIN MACAULEY
PUBLISHERS LTD.

A CIP catalogue record for this title is available from the British Library.

ISBN 9781785547546 (Paperback)
ISBN 9781785547553 (Hardback)
ISBN 9781785547560 (E-Book)

www.austinmacauley.com

First Published (2016)
Austin Macauley Publishers Ltd.
25 Canada Square
Canary Wharf
London
E14 5LQ

Acknowledgments

Like the book, I shall try to keep this short. My grateful thanks to the following:

- Graham Smedley, finance director extraordinaire, who also proved to be a talented copy editor;
- John Adair, who kindly reviewed the chapter on leadership;
- The late Dr Michael Reddy for reviewing the entire book and in particular the chapter on human capital management;
- Richard Smerdon, Jennifer Bryant-Pearson and Andrew Tyrie MP, who all helped in reviewing the chapter on corporate governance;
- Michael Cope for reviewing the chapter on compensation and benefits;
- Robert James Gerrard-Purse, my son, for his support and reviewing the chapter on resourcing;
- Alice Purse, my wife, for just being there;
- My publishers, for taking a leap of faith, and;
- All the people that I have worked and had conversations with over the years who made this book possible.

CONTENTS

FOREWORD

When I received a copy of the manuscript of this book, I assumed it to be yet another treatise on leadership vis-à-vis management. My natural instinct was to read it another day, somewhat complacent with my own attitude that there would be nothing radically new to read. As I started reading the book, I found myself stopping in my tracks. It is the simplicity and straightforwardness of what Robert says that got me to repeatedly stop and reflect on the applicability to my own businesses.

The Management of People is not a book on leadership, nor is it one on human resource management, or some fancy new management philosophy. It is simply a book that brings one back to the very basics of doing business. Somehow 21st century management literature assumes that the basics were over and done with in the previous century. It is like attempting to run modern software without updating the operating system itself.

We have all heard the adage 'leadership is doing the right things but management is doing them the right way'. To do something the right way implicitly holds that there must be some people to do them and then some universally accepted underlying principles that govern what that rightness is. These guiding principles are woven around five pillars of managerial interaction – Communication, Consistency, Dignity, Respect and Trust. The book reminds us of the age-old importance of communication with body language in the era of instant messaging and emails. The book is not against modern technology but rather builds on it by asking the most basic of questions; such as, why shouldn't one use Skype video instead of only audio when both come at the same price – free.

Corporate governance is the backbone to make organisations from good to great. However, it is inextricably linked with the management of people; for accountability and values will continue to be a very people-thing for the foreseeable future. The book draws examples from Robert's own varied career as well as other managers who were effective in managing people. It seeks to distinguish human capital management from human resources management without any overbearing use of semantics.

I am quite sure that this book shall be a great asset for managers who want to accomplish their organisational goals by way of engaging with people. The complete absence of managerial jargon and the easy flow of this book would qualify it to be called a page-turner, a rare feat for any management literature. It is an honour and a privilege to write the foreword and recommend this book to committed managers. This book would work as an operating system upon which many more management principles and practices can be built.

Anil Kariwala, CPA, CA
CEO, Kariwala Industries Ltd.
Calcutta
April 2015

PREFACE

This book is not about human resource management, of which more later, it is about the management of people. It is intended for a wide audience, from first-line supervisor to senior manager, indeed anyone with direct responsibility for the management of people. It will, I hope, also be of some interest to those specialists with little direct people management responsibility, but whose acts, or omissions, can have a massive impact upon an organisation's people. There is a chapter on leadership, but readers may be pleased to note that it does not contain yet another theory on leadership. The fundamentals of good people management are neither sector specific, nor are they country or culture specific, albeit, it is important to take account of the different customs and social attitudes that prevail in different cultures; they transcend (I believe) international boundaries and are equally applicable to any organisation that employs people, or is involved in the management of people:

- Public sector;
- Private sector;
- Private companies;
- Quoted companies;
- International companies;
- Multi-nationals;
- Charities;
- Not-for-profit organisations;
- Professional advisors, e.g. lawyers.

There are a number of recurring themes throughout the book, principally: Communication, Consistency, Dignity, Respect and Trust. It is my firm belief that if a manager, or organisation, gets these right then they are on the road to success. This book is primarily based upon my own personal experiences and recollections, but I have also drawn upon a wide range of books that I have read, together with conversations and experiences that I have been fortunate to have with some exceptional people.

The book is neither a textbook, nor does it provide any form of legal guidance, so it will not protect you from legal proceedings; however, if you, as a people manager, follow the principles set out in the book then that is a good starting point. Do what feels right, do what you honestly believe to be right and do it consistently. This does not always generate popularity, but it does tend to engender trust and respect.

This is not a textbook, but neither is it a novel that needs to be read in its entirety. Read and, I hope, enjoy those chapters that are of particular interest to you; if you enjoy some parts then you may be inclined to read others. The book does not provide a template and I am not convinced that a template for good people management exists, or ever will exist. Unlike machines, processes and systems, people do not fit into a set of Standard Operating Procedures. People think, they adapt, imagine, innovate and invent; they are your most important asset.

I hope that you find some value in the book and enjoy reading it, in whole, or in part, as much as I have enjoyed writing it. To paraphrase my friend Anil Kariwala, "I have tried my best to keep this book as concise as possible." This is partly because of my limited ability to write at length, but more significantly, my inability to read thick philosophical books end-to-end. So, I have applied the simple maxim – "Do not do to others what you do not want them to do to you." The book is unlikely to enter the *Sunday Times* 'Best

Seller' list, but I would very much welcome any comments, observations and suggestions at robert@robertpurse.co.uk.

INTRODUCTION

"Our people are our most important asset." How many times have you heard, or read, that statement? It invariably appears in the Chairman's Statement in the Annual Report and Accounts. Sadly, apart from the Remuneration Report, an organisation's people rarely get any further mention, except as a cost.

An organisation spends money on new equipment; that is an investment. The same organisation spends money on training people to operate the same new equipment; that is a cost. Clearly, I am missing something here. I go out and spend, for the sake of argument, £1.0M on a piece of equipment, e.g. a crane, so I have invested in a new crane that, in the due course of time, will find its way on to the asset register. The Marketing Department think this is wonderful; it will put us at the cutting edge. The accountants wax lyrically about the added value this crane will deliver. The Operations Department speaks of the operational efficiencies that the crane will deliver and the Sales Department talks of the competitive advantage that the new crane will deliver. All of this sounds wonderful, but there is a very large elephant in the room. If I do not 'invest' in training people to properly operate the crane just what do I have? I have a rapidly depreciating asset that delivers no added value whatsoever. It does not improve operational efficiency and it does not provide competitive advantage. The reality, I suggest, is that the crane of itself delivers no benefit whatsoever other than a new roost for pigeons and seagulls. The crane coupled with properly trained and motivated people is what delivers the benefits.

The same argument holds true across all sectors. You are the CEO of a National Health Service (NHS) Foundation Trust and the Trust board has voted unanimously in favour of acquiring a state of the art MRI scanner to enhance its diagnostic capabilities. You have never had this capability before, so you need to construct an appropriately equipped suite. Constructing the suite will cost c. £300k[1], which means that it is capital expenditure rather than revenue, so it is an investment. A whole body scanner is going to cost c. £1.9M. You, the Trust, have now spent about £2.2M at 2015 values, on a superb piece of modern technology that is worthless unless you have properly trained staff able to operate it and interpret the results. The cost of staff training is doubtless included in the project budget, but why is it a cost, rather than an investment? Given the requisite financial resources, any organisation can acquire state of the art equipment, facilities and systems. The key to making that investment a success is people. It is people that make the difference.

People are quite remarkable. Whilst we share with many other organisms the ability to learn and adapt, and have faculties that are no longer limited to the animal kingdom, (witness the developments in artificial intelligence and robotics that mean we now have machines capable of adapting, learning and, to a degree, communicating), for me, perhaps the most remarkable characteristics of people are the ability to:

- Think and reason;
- Create and communicate original, complex and sometimes abstract, concepts and ideas;
- Imagine;

---

[1] All costs are based upon 2015 prices.

- Innovate, test and adapt, and;
- Be self-determining and yet adaptive to the benefits of operating within a team.

Taken individually, it is possible that none of these characteristics is of itself unique to people. That being said, I would argue the point regarding the creation and communication of abstract concepts and ideas. These unique characteristics are enhanced by the variety of ways in which we can communicate. People can communicate through: body language (including facial expressions), pictures, speech and writing. Whilst these capabilities have doubtless been facilitated and potentially enhanced, to some degree, by technological advances, that same technology has also created hitherto unforeseen barriers to the effective management of people. Email, LinkedIn, Skype and Twitter are all important in their own right, but they do not provide the opportunity for real engagement with your people. Face-to-face, whether it is with an individual, or the team, is still best.

There are, for me, two other unique characteristics of people and those are the ability to treat others, irrespective of their position in the organisational hierarchy, with dignity and respect and the ability to give praise, where it is due, even when correcting errors. Praise can and should be public, criticism should not; to criticise one of your people in public is demeaning and denigrating, and will rarely, if ever, deliver a positive result.

CHAPTER 1

PEOPLE – YOUR MOST IMPORTANT ASSET

Whilst a cliché; this is also a self-evident truth. Perhaps more than ever before in today's knowledge-based economy, people really are your most important asset; it is an organisation's people that really make the difference in a knowledge economy. Take a look at any plc's Annual Report and Accounts, particularly the value of its fixed assets. Now look at the same plc's market capitalisation and then look at the difference between the two figures. You will quickly see there is something very significant missing and that something is intangible assets.

So what are intangible assets? Basically, they are things the accountants generally find difficult to measure. They are assets that are non-monetary in nature (or too variable to quantify in time and value), which are without physical substance. Intangible assets include:

- Intellectual property, e.g. business methodologies, copyrights, patents and trademarks;
- Customer lists and relationships;
- Licensing agreements;
- Brand recognition, think Coca-Cola;

- Computer software;
- Trade secrets;
- Reputation.

No mention, you will note, of people, no mention of an organisation's human capital. Where do many, perhaps most of these intangible assets originate from? They originate from people. Business methodologies are developed by people. Patents derive from original thinking, coupled with extensive research and development, by people. Computer software, customer relationships, musical works, trade secrets e.g. secret formulae, and reputation, ultimately they all derive from an organisation's people. Imagine what Manchester United would be worth without any players, or what Google would be worth without any software analysts, developers and engineers.

The issue of intangible assets is a significant problem for insolvency practitioners. In the past, when an organisation went into administration, there were often substantial fixed assets (buildings, equipment and plant) that could be sold. To a large extent, that no longer applies. Take, as an example, a facilities management company. It probably operates from leased or rented properties and the lease may well be terminated if the company goes into administration. Equipment and vehicles are probably leased, with a provision for termination if the company goes into administration. The same holds true for any contracts; clients invariably retain the right to terminate the contract in the event of the contractor going into administration. A consequence of this is that insolvency practitioners are now getting involved much earlier, while the organisation still has some value.

There is a potential downside to your people being your most important asset; they also represent your greatest liability, potentially an organisation's greatest source of risk. A cursory examination of the 2008 financial crisis may lead you to think that the root causes were:

- Collateralised debt obligations;
- Credit default swaps;
- Asset value bubbles;
- Futures contracts, and;
- Interest rate swaps.

Do you really understand all this jargon? No, well neither do I. The reality is that all these financial instruments were designed by people, they were approved by people (largely boards of directors, who did not understand what they were approving and rating agencies that should have), and they were implemented by people who were largely motivated/remunerated by short-term gains and lacked any effective oversight.

So let us have a few simple guidelines:

1. If you do not understand it, I mean really understand it, then do not do it,
2. If the benefits look too good to be true then they probably are. 'Get Poor Quick' schemes are far more common than successful 'Get Rich Quick' schemes.
3. Ensure that you have appropriate remuneration policies in place.
4. Ensure that you have an effective 'performance management' process. coupled with appropriate Key Performance Indicators (KPIs), and;
5. Establish a code of ethics/values and ensure that everyone (including the chairman) 'walks the talk'. Do what I say, but not what I do just does not work.

If you do not understand it then do not do it!

I use a simple 'rule of thumb': If it takes more than two A4 pages (one is ideal) to summarise a proposition then I start to get suspicious. The summary should include a cost/benefit analysis and a risk assessment; whatever the nature of the proposition, there are always risks and they may not always be obvious! A cheaper source of supply may, at first sight, make commercial sense, but what happens if your new supplier is using child labour? What happens if your supplier is sourcing materials from dubious sources? Think horsemeat, think Rana Plaza, the reputational damage was immense. All too often risk is seen as a purely financial issue. Financial risk is an important piece of the jigsaw puzzle, but it is arguable that people risk is of equal, if not greater, importance.

Ensure that you have appropriate remuneration policies in place.

This applies from the board down. So what are appropriate remuneration policies? Let us start with what they are not. Remuneration policies should not be short-termist. Short-termism, the abject failure to take the long-term view, underpinned a lot of the causes of the latest financial crisis. You do not load your remuneration policies so that everyone's focus is on short-term gains. Earnings per Share (EPS) is a commonly accepted measure for executive bonus schemes, but it is susceptible to manipulation. Have you ever wondered about the popularity of share buy-back schemes? Well, wonder no more; if a company buys back shares then there are fewer shares in circulation, which means greater EPS and bigger bonuses for the directors. Short-termism is by no means restricted to the 'Great and Good'. A salesperson secures a new piece of business, which is good news and he/she should receive some reward. The bad news is that after bonuses, cost of sales, discounts and the like it is conceivable that you made a loss on the initial deal. The key here is retaining and, if possible, increasing the new business in the years to come, which means taking a longer-term focus.

So what are the characteristics of appropriate remuneration policies?

a. Keep them simple. In common with most, if not all policies, they should be easy to understand. If it requires the services of an HR professional, or lawyer, to interpret them then your policies are not fit for purpose; scrap them and start again. This principle should apply at all levels in the organisation.

b. If your board has a remuneration committee, it is worth looking at how many, if any, of its members have practical experience of constructing remuneration/reward policies for senior executives. If the answer is none then the board becomes almost totally reliant upon external advisors, advisors who will rarely, if ever, advise a pay freeze, or below 'average' award. Why? Because they like their annual repeat fees and since they are probably recommended/selected by the CEO or CFO they are not going to make recommendations that adversely affect his, or her, package (turkeys, and Christmas comes to mind).

c. Ensure that policies are fair and equitable. It is a fact that people talk about what they are paid. Please do not waste your time telling people not to discuss their pay and benefits with colleagues; such an approach will create suspicion and the discussion is going to happen anyway. If your policies are not fair and equitable people will find out and you will either lose good people, or you will have people who feel under-valued, or end up defending an 'equal pay' claim. In all cases the result is financial and reputational damage to your organisation. Make sure that the executive team does not receive improvements in their remuneration when all other employees are subject to a pay freeze. In this context, executive team very definitely applies to all sectors, private and public (politicians please note!).

d. Avoid incremental pay scales like the plague. The fact that someone has been doing a job for 10 years, does not, of itself, mean that they are more effective and efficient than someone who has been doing the same job for two years. Age, gender and length of service have no place in a remuneration policy. Performance is what counts

e. Make sure that your policies are linked to both business and individual performance, which leads nicely into the subject of performance management.

Ensure that you have an effective 'performance management' process.

Yes, performance management is about people, but it is not just about performance appraisals/reviews. performance management involves:

1. Learning and development;
2. Organisation design and effectiveness, and;
3. Performance review and improvement.

I suggest that we look at the performance review first. Performance review/appraisal is not an annual 'tick box' exercise. It is an on-going process, throughout the year or appraisal cycle, that should ensure a clear understanding of:

- What the individual's job involves;

- How the job fits into the organisation and how it contributes to the success of the team and ultimately the organisation;
- What the key objectives/outputs are and how they will be measured;
- How they have done over the review period, and;
- What additional assistance, skills, support and resources does the job-holder need to achieve success?

The last point is crucial, particularly during periods of significant change. If you, the line manager, do not ensure that the individual has the assistance, skills, support and resources that the job holder needs to do the job properly then the failure is yours, not theirs. Wherever possible, this should be pro-active, rather than reactive. Taking my earlier analogies, if you have already decided to acquire the new crane, or MRI scanner, that is the time to identify the people who will operate the equipment. It is also the time to plan their training. This can be a very cost-effective stratagem; you can make the purchase conditional upon the supplier providing the necessary training for the people who are to operate it. An additional benefit is that your people will see real evidence of your commitment to developing and enhancing their skills, which is likely to improve employee engagement and motivation; it may also improve employee retention.

Some Points to Remember

1.	Always ensure people have good notice of a review meeting.
2.	Encourage your people to prepare for review meetings.
3.	This is a private meeting, so do ensure that a suitable room is made available and, unless WWIII is about to be declared, no interruptions.
4.	Turn your mobile off and suggest that your colleague does the same.
5.	Allow sufficient time.
6.	Do make notes during a review meeting; human memory is far from perfect and relying on it, perhaps months after the event, can be very risky.
7.	Do a brief note (bullet points are fine) after the meeting and send it to your colleague to ensure a shared understanding.
8.	Please ensure that your note identifies any critical success factors (e.g. resources, agreed outcomes and timescales).

Table 1
Performance Review Checklist

As already mentioned, a performance review is not simply an annual exercise; it is an ongoing process, which means that when you get to the end of the appraisal cycle, there should be few, if any surprises. Organisations are dynamic; they have to constantly adapt to changing circumstances and priorities. The same is true of their people, but they need to understand the changes if they are to effectively adapt to them and successfully meet the new challenges. Another significant benefit from having a structured approach to performance review is that it aids consistency of treatment for all the people in an organisation.

Understanding what the individual's job involves may sound like a statement of the blindingly obvious, but it isn't. Both manager and job holder need to have a shared understanding of what the job is. You should both have copies of a job description, but you may well interpret it in different ways. Added to which, the job description might not reflect changed circumstances and priorities. I am still amazed at the number of times that I have been involved in disciplinary proceedings where it was quite clear that the job holder and line manager did not have a shared understanding of what the job involved.

How the job fits into the organisation and how it contributes to the success of the team/organisation is an interesting issue. There is a story, possibly/probably apocryphal, about the late President Kennedy talking to a cleaner at Cape Canaveral. The President apparently asked the cleaner what his job was. The cleaner's answer was quite simple, "My job is to help put a man on the moon." With just a little bit of thought even the most menial of jobs can be given a wider context.

Organisation design and effectiveness are key elements of performance management. As an organisation adapts and evolves, so must its structures and processes if it is to remain fit for purpose. A tip here, why not ask your people how the organisation could be better structured to enable it to work smarter and empower them to do their job better and be more effective? Do this and you are not only involving them, but also empowering them. Involving them means that they are much more likely to take some ownership of the new structure and processes; empowering them shows that you respect their views and opinions. Good leaders do empowerment, 'toxic' leaders do not. It will probably (almost certainly) be a slower process than you might prefer, but eventually the results will justify your commitment. Yes, there may well be some pretty unrealistic suggestions, but take the time to explain why those suggestions are not practicable, it not only shows that you have considered them, it shows that you value input from your people and that you will not 'put them down' because a suggestion is unworkable. If you constantly seek to improve the design and effectiveness of your organisation, or your part of it, then it becomes part of an evolutionary/incremental process. So talk to your people/ask your people about:

- How can we reduce waste;
- How can we reduce down time/waiting time;
- How can we reduce energy consumption, and;
- How can we improve the client/customer experience, which includes both internal and external clients/customers?

How they have done over the review period? Your people deserve/need to know how they are doing on a regular basis; there should be no surprises at the Annual Review. If someone has done really well during the year, then praise them publicly and at the time; not in private months later. Years ago there was a delightful 'Peanuts' or 'Dilbert' cartoon that went something along these lines, "Working here is like wetting your pants in a dark cupboard; it gives you a warm feeling yet nobody notices." If they are not doing well tell them privately and explain what is required to rectify the situation, agree an action plan, outputs and timescales; ideally, end the conversation on a positive note.

You do not need to create (performance review) documentation from scratch. ACAS produces some first class documents[2] that you can always tailor to your specific needs/requirements.

Learning and development are not 'nice to have', they are essential. I have seen a number of economic downturns (recessions) and invariably the first budget to be cut is learning and development (training). I have yet to hear a single convincing reason for cutting expenditure (investment) on learning and development. Cutting learning and development costs increases the probability that your organisation's future productive capability will be damaged, since the 'costs' that you are cutting are, in

---

[2] http://www.acas.org.uk/index.aspx?articleid=1438

reality, the investments that your organisation needs to make for future success. As we come out of a recession, one of the first and loudest complaints is, "We haven't got enough skilled people." Really, and who is to blame? Amazingly if you do not train people, especially apprentices and graduate trainees, in an economy with an ageing working population then you will end up with a skill shortage! In the RICS UK Construction Market Survey for Q3 of 2014[3], 59 per cent of respondents cited labour shortages as a limitation on higher growth in activity. Many years ago (in the late 1970s) I worked for a company called Rank Hi Fi and we trained more apprentices and graduate engineers than we needed to. My MD's (Malcolm Holt's) philosophy was quite simple and fully supported by his then personnel manager (Chris Briody): "If we train them well, treat them well and keep in touch then they will come back when a suitable opportunity arises."

Investment in learning and development is an investment in the future of your organisation. 'Employer of choice' is a phrase that is frequently heard from employers and HR professionals nowadays. It seems to me that investing in the learning and development of your people is a major step in the journey towards becoming an employer of choice.

Be consistent in the way you treat your people. Forget disability, ethnicity, gender, race and religion; they are all people and everyone deserves to be treated in the same way and subject to the same standards. Disability, I am partially disabled myself, doesn't mean treating a disabled person differently, in fact, most disabled people would find that really offensive; it simply means making a few, very often minor, adjustments to enable them to do their job properly. The standards are the same as those expected/required of any able-bodied employee in the same role, albeit, subject to the needs of the job. There can be reasonable

---

[3] http://www.rics.org & economics@rics.org

adjustments (support arrangements) made for the disabled that neither denigrate the individual, nor undermine the above principle.

Ethnicity and race are not good grounds for different treatment, nor were they ever. Religion, I write as someone with a fairly strong dislike for 'organised' religion, is not a special case. Religion has arguably been the cause of more deaths, wars, suffering and mutilation than any other cause in the history of mankind. Every one of your people is entitled to their own personal beliefs and faith, but there are some areas where I have a real concern. If someone wants to proselytise that is fine, provided they do it in their own time, not at work, and it does not bring your organisation into disrepute. If someone wants to wear a symbol of their faith then, provided that it is safe for them and others to do so, why not? I do draw the line at the full face veil; setting aside my personal view that it is indicative to me of female subjugation, it serves to conceal and that creates a barrier to effective communication, identification and response recognition. There is extensive research to confirm this. Professor Albert Mehrabian[4] pioneered the understanding of communications. He is Professor Emeritus of Psychology, UCLA, and his work featured strongly in the mid to late 1990s in establishing an understanding of body language and non-verbal communications. Mehrabian's research provided the basis for the widely quoted statistic for the effectiveness of spoken communications. His findings were, in brief, that:

- 7 per cent of message pertaining to feelings and attitudes is in the words that are spoken.
- 38 per cent of message pertaining to feelings and attitudes is paralinguistic (the way that the words are said).

---

[4] Professor Albert Mehrabian www.kaaj.com/psych

- 55 per cent of message pertaining to feelings and attitudes is in facial expression.

I am aware that Mehrabian's work[5] relates specifically to communications of feelings and attitudes, but intuitively and based upon personal experience I am convinced that it has great relevance to the whole business of communicating with your people. The value of Mehrabian's theory relates to communications where emotional content is significant, and the need to understand it properly is great, which is often applicable in people management, where motivation and attitude have a crucial effect on outcomes.

So how do you treat your people? The short answer is that you treat them as you would expect and hope to be treated yourself; you treat them with dignity and respect. Treating people with dignity and respect pays dividends. Some years ago I was involved in 'exiting' a senior manager, who had been somewhat imprudent in his dealings with a female colleague, from a plc. Not many months after he offered me an assignment. Yes, I had the skills that he was looking for, but equally important to him I had treated him with dignity and respect.

This principle does not just apply to existing employees; it also applies to potential employees (job applicants). You, all of us, would be wise to remember that the applicant we are rejecting today may, at some point in the future, be our manager, or potential customer and people do have long memories. I am currently considering non-executive director opportunities and I have been amazed and disappointed by the number of organisations (almost entirely private sector) that simply lack the good manners to acknowledge formal enquiries and proposals.

---

[5] Mehrabian, A. (1981). *Silent Messages: Implicit communication of emotions and attitudes*. Belmont, CA: Wadsworth (currently distributed by Albert Mehrabian, am@kaaj.com)

Well, if you treat potential board appointments like that then how do you treat people lower down the food chain? Not very well I suspect, which does not say anything good about your (organisation's) approach to people management. I am no apologist for the public sector, but their approach to recruitment and selection is open, transparent and invariably well managed.

There is another category of employee that is worthy of particular mention; those under threat of, or under notice of, termination by reason of redundancy. Terminating someone's employment, unless under the most exceptional of circumstances, is never easy; if you ever find it becoming so then perhaps you should consider a career change. People under threat of redundancy are invariably in that situation because of circumstances entirely beyond their direct control, which may include a range of factors such as:

- Economic recession;
- Changes in market demand;
- Changes in technology;
- A change in strategic direction;
- Management incompetence;
- Outsourcing;
- Relocation, and;
- An acquisition or merger.

Because the people concerned are being affected by matters outside their control, you must expect a fair degree of anger and hostility when you are talking to them/consulting with them. Redundancy consultation, whether individual or collective, is not a 'tick box' exercise, you are dealing with real people not numbers. When circumstances change in the future, you may have need of the very people that are made redundant, so you should always treat them with dignity and respect; do not simply plan the redundancy, but also plan for life afterwards.

The law[6] in the UK currently requires you to undertake collective consultation when you are proposing 20, or more, redundancies at a single establishment and it sets out the process to be adopted. All of this is fine, but what happens if you are an SME employing 150 people and you propose making 15 redundancies? That is 10 per cent of your workforce (at Tesco that would be approaching 50,000 people). Technically, you do not have to undertake collective consultation, but I suggest that you do; this level of staff reduction is almost certainly going to impact all of your people. When undertaking consultation, do listen to your people's suggestions; you may be pleasantly surprised. Some years ago I was involved in a fairly major redundancy and one of the departments that was probably going to be affected was R&D. The staff of the R&D department asked for a meeting and, in brief, their proposition was:

- ➢ We work as a team.
- ➢ We do good work (they were acknowledged industry experts in their field).
- ➢ Our work is important for the future of the organisation.
- ➢ We will all take a voluntary 10 per cent cut in salary if it means that we can keep the existing team in place.

Their proposal was not one that the management team had considered and if we had then I suspect that we would have dismissed it as unrealistic. Needless to say, we did adopt their suggestion and it worked. You do not have to agree with everything that your people say/suggest, they would not expect you to, but do listen to what they have to

---

[6] Trade Union and Labour Relations Act (TULRA) 1992

say. You, the board, the management team, do not know everything!

Where collective consultation is involved, UK law sets out minimum consultation periods. These are currently:

- Where 20, or more, redundancies are proposed at a single establishment 30 days, and;
- Where 100, or more, redundancies are proposed at a single establishment 45 days.

If there are no recognised trade unions these timescales may be realistic, albeit I have my doubts. Employee representatives need to consult with the people that they represent and they need to get a mandate from their people, which takes time. If there are trade unions involved, I think that the timescales are not realistic, particularly with regard to large-scale redundancies. Trade union officials are very busy people and they are also, as a rule, very professional. They will need to:

- Change their diaries;
- Consider the employer's proposals;
- Consult with elected representatives;
- Consult with the members, and;
- Secure a clear mandate.

The situation becomes even more complicated where there is more than one recognised trade union. I was involved in one small (30 posts at risk) redundancy, where there were four recognised trade unions; arranging meetings was a nightmare! Another thing to remember about collective consultation is that it has to be meaningful and undertaken with a view to reaching agreement. If you fail to disclose relevant information, or simply prevaricate then you could end up with a 'Protective Award' being made against your organisation. There is something of a myth about collective consultation that suggests the consultation periods are set in tablets of stone. Undoubtedly the law does establish the minimum duration, but it does not establish a maximum. If you are approaching the end of the minimum period, but agreement looks like a realistic probability, then what do you really lose by extending consultation slightly? If nothing else, you have shown that your organisation was willing to 'go the extra mile' in the hope of reaching agreement.

Organisation design and effectiveness are integral to the performance management process. As an organisation develops and evolves, so should its structure. As the market changes and evolves and the needs of clients/customers change, so must the organisation. Such changes need not, save in exceptional circumstances, be revolutionary, but it should be on-going; as Sir John Harvey-Jones[7] is reputed to have said, "Change is the status quo." Every organisation needs to be constantly looking for ways to improve its effectiveness and respond to changes in the market in which it operates. Some years ago I worked for an organisation whose principal activity was meat; specifically the production, processing, wholesaling and retailing of meat (bacon, beef, chicken, lamb, pork, and et cetera). The company was a global empire, but such was the level of vertical integration that only the retail arm actually generated profit, which was fine until the supermarkets started selling fresh meat. The retail operation went into 'freefall' and, because the other businesses had never operated on a strictly commercial (arm's length) basis, so did the other businesses. Such is the fate of organisations and their people that fail to respond to the changing needs of the market.

Another important element of organisation effectiveness is succession planning, with the emphasis on planning. Your organisation's performance management

---

[7] Sir John Harvey-Jones b.16.4.1924, d.9.1.2008

process should identify people with the potential for further development/promotion. Identifying the potential is just one step in the process; that potential needs to be developed. Learning and development activities have their place here, but so too does mentoring. Mentoring your own people is difficult, but not impossible. It may conflict with your role as a line manager and requires a high degree of trust and openness. Very often the best/most effective mentors come from a different discipline or department to that of the 'mentee'. This provides the mentee with a broader perspective and a better understanding of activities outside her/his day-to-day work. Mentoring can require a significant time commitment from the mentor, so mentors need to be selected with care.

Gaining a broader perspective is probably more important now than it has ever been. In the past, many people started their working lives as 'generalists' and specialised later. That is no longer the case; people tend to specialise very early in their career, and often when at college, or university; thus someone intent upon a career in HR, IT, or Marketing, will invariably have studied that subject before entering the job market. This has its merits, particularly for employers, as it reduces the need for 'on-the-job' training before the new employee can make a positive contribution to their organisation. However, it can also have its demerits:

- It encourages a 'silo' mentality, whereby people see themselves as part of a department/function, rather than part of an organisation;
- People are, generally, less able to see their work and the impact that it may have in a broader organisational context, and;
- People can be less well equipped to move into a general management role.

26

To a degree, the situation has been aggravated by business schools and universities offering 'focussed' general management and MBA courses. I accept that these institutions want to differentiate themselves from the competition, but I am at something of a loss to understand why, a general management course would have a particular (functional) focus. General management courses that I have attended, all without a functional focus, have benefited from having delegates with a wide range of experience, gained in different sectors. Perhaps the best of these courses was the Senior Course at Henley Management College, now Henley Business School[8] and part of Reading University, where there were people from both different sectors and different countries. The courses run by the Institute of Directors[9] (IoD) come a close second.

---

[8] http://henley.ac.uk/
[9] http://www.iod.com/

CHAPTER 2

LEARNING AND DEVELOPMENT

The ability to learn is an essential attribute of organisations and their people in today's knowledge-based economy, but in common with most investments it requires a longer-term focus where you balance short-term costs against long-term returns. In common with the other investments that an organisation makes, investment in learning and development should demonstrate a quantifiable benefit, a positive return on investment (ROI), that needs to be measured to ensure that you're learning and development activities are (cost) effective. Measuring that ROI should not be limited to direct benefits; there is considerable evidence to suggest that investing in your people through learning and development can result in significant reductions in unwanted staff turnover.

A short programme of training, whether in-house or external, may well produce significant short-term gains. Very often breaking a programme up into a series of modules (bite size chunks) can be very useful; it gives your people the opportunity to fully absorb and then apply what they have learned in a practical work context before undertaking the next module. There is an added advantage in that your people are only out of the work environment for short (manageable) periods of time, so they focus on the learning activity rather than worrying about work. I have found this approach to be particularly useful with first-line (junior) supervisors and managers. There can also be some unforeseen advantages:

On one occasion I was asked to design and implement a modular programme for 1st line managers that was to be run on-site; we were fortunate in having a well-equipped training facility. The catch was cost; we wanted to use trainers who really knew their subject and its practical application. We secured the services of trainers used by the Engineering Employers' Federation[10] and we could guarantee at least five delegates per module. The trainers' preference was for 8–10 delegates. The answer was simplicity itself; I contacted other local employers and asked if they would like to take advantage of any 'spare' places that we had. They would and they did with the result that each module had at least eight delegates, which helped us in two ways. Firstly, we got some useful revenue that reduced the impact on the training budget. Secondly, and perhaps more importantly, the mix of delegates from different industries enriched the entire programme.

Apprenticeships and graduate trainee programmes represent by their very nature a longer-term investment, but there can also be medium-term benefits to be gained. If/when your organisation gains a reputation for running good apprenticeship and graduate training schemes; it increases your attractiveness to potential employees and gives you a competitive advantage over your competitors.

Effective learning and development makes your organisation and its people more adaptable and better able to respond positively to change. Many formal learning and development activities can be derived directly from your performance review processes, part of which should

---

[10] www.eef.org.uk

include creating a Personal Development Plan (PDP). The PDP should not only identify the activity, but also how and when it is to be delivered and what the outcomes (benefits) will be. Learning and development is not limited to formal activities, informal activities can be just as important, particularly when the dividing line between work and learning and development is becoming increasingly blurred. If you need to quickly find some information that will help you with your work a search on the internet will invariably help you to find the information you require. If you work in an organisation that operates a well-maintained intranet, a quick search may well reveal that you have a subject expert in-house; I do emphasise well maintained, there are some organisations that have difficulty in even maintaining an accurate internal telephone list. Such informal learning is increasingly common and it is difficult to differentiate between informal learning and work. One note of caution here; if your people are allowed access to the intranet, there needs to be a clear understanding of the rules for usage.

CHAPTER 3

COMMUNICATION

Effective communication is not simply important, it is essential for any manager, or organisation. Effective communication is essential to good people management. Forget the likes of the 'ICE' regulations[11]; no matter how well meaning, Government cannot legislate, or regulate, communication with your people. Good communication is good for your business; talking to your people shows that they are valued and that they are involved. To use an analogy, communication is the lubrication that enables the organisation's machinery to work. There is an expression, "Nature abhors a vacuum." If you do not communicate with your people then you are encouraging rumour and the grape-vine[12] to fill the communication vacuum. If, on the other hand, you regularly communicate – ideally face to face – with your people then you will gain their trust and their respect.

---

[11] The Information and Consultation of Employees Regulations 2004 (Statutory Instrument 2004 No. 3426), which now apply to any organisation with at least 50 employees.
[12] There is an excellent video on this subject produced by Video Arts (http://www.videoarts.com) in 1996.

Effective communication does not necessarily require training, albeit training can and does help, above all effective communication requires honesty, openness and sincerity. Communication training can help you to better understand your audience. It can help you avoid irritating habits such as playing with the keys in your pocket and it can help you realise the importance of looking at your audience, not at your notes. In any programme for newly appointed/potential managers, do include a module on communication.

All of this does not mean that you have to tell everyone everything, but if you cannot disclose something then say so; unless extreme circumstances preclude that, do not prevaricate. Honesty is definitely the best policy when it comes to communication!

I accept that email, Skype, Twitter, texting and the like have their place, but I do not accept that they represent effective communication. Do remember Professor Mehrabian's research, referred to earlier. Email has immediacy, but that isn't everything. You cannot ask an email a question; you cannot ask an email for clarification. By the time you have finished, you may as well have had a telephone conversation, or better still a face-to-face conversation, or meeting. How many times have you received emails from someone in the same office as you? How many times have you sent emails to someone in the same office as you? Why not just walk over to them and have a conversation? You can then see their reaction to what you are saying and vice versa.

Email does provide an electronic 'paper trail', but that also brings its own hazards; unless they are covered by legal privilege, emails are discoverable in legal proceedings; there is no such thing as a private email, as many politicians and senior business executives have found to their cost! Never send an email that would cause you embarrassment if it were made public. I did and needless to say the recipient made it public. The recipient was a full-time trade union officer (FTO) and this was the only occasion I have ever had an FTO disclose a confidential communication.

Another problem with email that links to its immediacy is the almost overwhelming urge to respond and quickly. Is World War III going to be declared if you do not respond straight away? Is your organisation going into administration if you do not respond straight away? I rather hope that the answer to both questions is no, so why not stop and think? There is an old adage that says, "Engage brain before opening mouth." In the case of emails, it should probably be, "Engage brain before pressing the send button." Sensitive and potentially emotive subjects justify saving your email as a draft, going back to it later, reviewing and perhaps amending it and then sending it. I have on occasion (as former colleagues will agree) sent some emails that were, to put it mildly, lacking in subtlety, tact and diplomacy.

I am rather partial to Skype, which does at least permit direct and visual contact with your correspondent(s), but can someone please explain to me why so many people avoid the use of video on Skype? If someone consciously avoids the use of video that could be interpreted as hiding, or seeking to hide, something. Rather pointless really since they probably have a photograph posted on their LinkedIn profile and may well have a video on their website.

Twitter is okay, but a 140-character limit is not exactly conducive to a meaningful exchange of views and opinions. It is constraining to the point of being dangerous if a relatively nuanced exchange is required. I welcome electronic communication, indeed I welcome any medium that encourages communication, but for me, effective communication involves a number of characteristics:

- Communication is about talking to people, not at them.
- Communication is a dialogue, not a diatribe. It is a two-way process.
- Effective communication offers people an opportunity to ask questions, to get clarification and minimise confusion and misunderstandings.
- Effective communication offers an opportunity to canvas people's opinions and views and, ideally, their emotional response.

1.	Primarily to enable and improve downward, upward and sideways communication throughout the organisation.
2.	To prevent the 'grapevine' from gaining credibility.
3.	To ensure that there is clarity of direction and information throughout the organisation.
4.	To provide a forum for asking questions and making suggestions that can/must be promptly responded to by senior managers.

Table 2
Why Communicate?

I am a great advocate of Team Briefings and, unless we are talking about a 'micro-business', I think the general principles are applicable to any organisation. Team Briefing was developed by the Industrial Society, now the Work Foundation.[13] The core purpose of Team Briefing[14] is described in Table 2.

---

[13] The Work Foundation http://www.theworkfoundation.com

To the above table, which is far from comprehensive, I would add the following:

Team Briefings give everyone in the team an opportunity to understand what the other team members are doing and understand the impact of their work on co-workers.

How often should you hold Team Briefings? I do not believe that there is a single answer to this question. I think that the consensus is either weekly, or monthly, but it depends on a range of variables such as:

- The size of the organisation;
- Its structure and complexity, and;
- Recent developments involving internal and external changes (including media reports).

My suggestion is to ask your people how often, unless there is a major development, they think Team Briefings should routinely take place. In my experience, you will get sensible suggestions. Do remember that some of your people may work from home, or work part-time, so take this into account when arranging your briefings and do ensure that anyone in your team who is unable to attend (through holiday, illness, maternity leave, et cetera.) is provided with a summary of what was discussed. How long should briefings last? If they are held weekly then 30 minutes is probably sufficient. If monthly then an hour is probably more realistic, but there is no stock answer.

What issues should you address?

- **Progress** – How the company/team is doing, how we are performing against our objectives, any

---

[14] This book is not about Team Briefing, but there is a lot of information available on the topic. Not least from http://www.businessballs.com

barriers to progress and remember to celebrate success.

- **Plans** – What is the company/team committed to achieving over the next week/month, any significant forthcoming events.
- **People** – Any significant people events/issues. Address rumours only when they have the potential to affect/demoralise any of your stakeholders.
- **Problems** – Any 'big ticket' issues that need attention.

Do encourage input from all your people, some will be more reticent than others, but everyone should be actively encouraged to contribute. Remember that this is a business meeting, not a social occasion. That being said, the two can sometimes be usefully combined, particularly if your people are widely dispersed. In one organisation where I worked, the HR Department was not all under one roof and included: employee relations, HR administration, learning and development (including technical training), and payroll. We agreed that the best solution was to have monthly team briefings held outside normal office hours. The biggest nightmare was organising the food (we had Christians, Hindus, Muslims and vegetarians). If you are going to run a management conference then I suggest no more than once, or twice, a year; otherwise it could be interpreted as a management 'jolly'. Northern Rail used to run an excellent annual management conference, under the leadership of Heidi Mottram, the then MD.

When structuring your communication arrangements, such as team briefings, do not forget to take account of your people who are: home-based, job-sharing, part-time, or mobile.

CHAPTER 4

LEADERSHIP

There are some people who argue that the 'leadership' of people is quite separate and distinct from the management of people, I disagree. For me they are two sides of the same coin; a truly effective leader must be able to manage their people and a truly effective manager must provide leadership to their people; a good leader may not be a good manager, in which case the leader needs to recognise this shortcoming and ensure that he/she has good managers to compensate. The best leaders are good managers and the best managers are also good leaders. Some, perhaps many, of you will be pleased to see that I do not have the temerity, or arrogance to come up with yet another theory on leadership. In many cases the majority of theorists have, at best, a tenuous link to practical leadership, possibly no better than that of Lewis Carroll (See below). The late Dr Michael Reddy (my former chairman at HPA Group and someone I held in high esteem) was quite disparaging about the many and various leadership models and theories that keep emerging. As an example, I was recently amazed to discover that the National Health Service in the UK has now developed its own Leadership Model. I cannot help thinking that the NHS has more important priorities than re-inventing the wheel. For my part, I prefer theorists who have, to use common parlance: been there, seen it and done it. I will, however, start this section with a quotation from someone who probably lacked any practical experience whatsoever of leadership:

"If you don't know where you are going, any road will get you there." – Lewis Carroll (Charles Lutwidge Dodgson) 1832–1898

Way back, in the 1970s, when I was undertaking my Army Officer training, I was introduced to a model of leadership that resonated with me then and still holds true, for me at least, today. A minor digression, but probably a worthwhile one: when I left the Army I found that many quite senior managers thought that leadership in the Armed Forces amounted to little more than giving orders and shouting at people. That might (I emphasise 'might') have been true of Wellington's army in the early 19th century, but it is certainly not true of the UK's post-National Service armed forces. Save for a, thankfully, small number of zealots and fanatics, no one deliberately puts themselves in harm's way without good reason. It requires leadership of the very highest degree, which is why our Armed Forces take leadership very seriously.

Back to my preferred model of leadership, it was originated by a chap called John Adair[15] and is now generally referred to as 'Action-Centred Leadership'. At its core, it is simple, easy to understand and free of psychobabble; these attributes make a good starting point. The major benefit is that it works and it works in every type of organisation that I have been involved with. My view on the constant stream of new models and theories of leadership is quite straightforward; I am using a model developed by someone with practical experience of leadership. It worked 40 years ago and still works. It isn't

---

[15] http://www.johnadair.co.uk/

broken, so why would I want to change it or fix it? Adair's work undoubtedly encompasses and incorporates concepts developed by Herzberg, Maslow and others, but it clearly demonstrates that leadership is a trainable and transferable skill. It is not an exclusively inborn psychological characteristic. That being said, there are doubtless some personality traits that mean that some people may be more 'naturally' inclined to leadership roles than others. There are also people who possess personality traits that are commonly found among psychopaths; a combination of the two sets of traits would indeed be a cause for concern, leading to what might well be called 'toxic leadership'..

Leadership is not gender-specific, which is a point worth bearing in mind when you are involved in recruitment. If you are short on names of great female leaders, here are a few:

- Aethelflaed (c.864–918) – Daughter of Alfred the Great, known as 'The Lady of Mercia';
- Boudicca (d. AD 60 or 61);
- Catherine the Great (1729– 1796);
- Elizabeth I (1533–1603);
- Helena Rubenstein (1872–1965);
- Margaret Thatcher (1925–2013);
- Aung San Suu Kyi (1945–), and;
- Ginni Rometty (1957–) – CEO of IBM.

I have not included Queen Elizabeth II because as a constitutional monarch she no longer leads our country, supposedly the Government does.

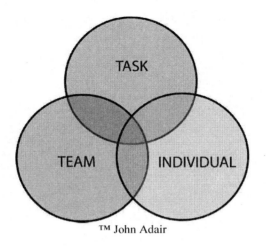

™ John Adair

Figure 1
Action-Centred Leadership

The 'Action-Centred Leadership' model,[16] developed by John Adair, is represented by the 'three circles' diagram shown above. The interlinked circles show the interdependence of the three areas of:

- Achieving the task;
- Managing the team (team maintenance), and;
- Managing the individual members of the team.

If you obscure one of the circles, the other two are left incomplete. For example if you obscure the task i.e. there is no defined task, or there is a failure to achieve it, this will adversely impact both team maintenance/management and individual satisfaction.

---

[16] *Action Centred Leadership* (John Adair) first published 1973.

Leaders at all levels and in all organisations need to provide their people with:

- ✓ Clarity of purpose (a defined objective);
- ✓ A plan for the team and individual team members (clear direction);
- ✓ Clearly defined timescales, quality standards and reporting arrangements;
- ✓ Individual and team accountabilities and responsibilities;
- ✓ The skills to do the job;
- ✓ The equipment to do the job;
- ✓ The materials to do the job;
- ✓ Encouragement and enthusiasm; and,
- ✓ The resilience and adaptability to respond, without losing focus, to the unforeseen.

Effective leadership also involves the delegation of authority and empowerment. Unwillingness on the part of leaders to delegate authority, or empower their people, implies a lack of trust in their people (including subordinate leaders). This sort of 'toxic' leadership can sometimes be found in so-called charismatic leaders.

The next vital step is to check that your people have a clear, shared, understanding of the issues covered; you should never assume that everyone understands. Shared understanding is important for two principal reasons:

First, everyone understands the contribution their work makes towards achieving the objective, and; second, your people will realise that it is a team effort and only if everyone supports each other and works cooperatively with other team members will a successful outcome be achieved.

This all sounds like fairly basic stuff, which it is, but it applies to every team in any organisation from the board of directors, or equivalent, down. It also provides a useful indicator of where accountability/responsibility lies. The leader is responsible for ensuring that all team members have the skills required. The leader is also responsible for ensuring that their people have the equipment and materials needed, and the leader is accountable for achieving overall success. I address the issue of accountability in more detail in the chapter on Corporate Governance; suffice to say that I cannot see how it is possible to have good corporate governance without accountability and values. This list incidentally also provides the framework for a performance management process, which is covered in more detail in the chapter on human resources management.

To be a really effective leader/people manager, you need to be self-aware; you need to understand yourself and how the various aspects of your preferred/typical leadership style (good and not so good) can impact on your people and affect their performance. You also need to have an understanding of your direct reports.

I firmly believe that every leader/manager would benefit from a full personality profile of themselves, such as the Fifteen Factor Questionnaire (15FQ),[17] 16PF,[18] or Occupational Personality Questionnaire (OPQ).[19] There are many such personality measures available, but please never use one that has not been subject to proper peer review. The British Psychological Society (www.bps.co.uk) has a wealth of information on this topic. The late Professor Paul Kline produced an excellent book (*The Handbook of Psychological Testing* – published 1995 by Routledge) that is well worth a read. When it comes to gaining a (better) understanding of your preferred/typical leadership, or management style, there are many 'type' indicators available and I have found both the Jung Type Indicator (JTI™) and the Myers-Briggs Type Indicator (MBTI™)

---

[17] 15 Factor Questionnaire – http://www.uk.psytech.com
[18] 16 Personality Factor Questionnaire - http://www.ipat.com
[19] OPQ – http://www.ceb.shl.com

very useful. Personality Measures and Type Indicators should only be administered and interpreted by qualified practitioners. In the UK, the best guide to qualified practitioners is available through the British Psychological Society's (BPS) Register of Qualifications in Test Use (RQTU). The BPS can probably also provide advice on appropriate regulatory bodies outside the UK.

Good self-awareness and a better understanding of the people in your team should result in improved results and can be very productive in the context of improving overall team and individual performance. I firmly believe that truly successful teams need a mix of people with different personality types. Having a board, or chief executive's team, made up of people sharing largely the same personality characteristics/type may give everyone a nice warm glow, but it can also, in the absence of constructive challenge and criticism, lead to 'Group Think'.[20] As a leader, gaining agreement through consensus is good provided that proposals are subject to careful scrutiny.

A better (shared) understanding of your team and the individuals that make it up facilitates better understanding and greater respect between all team members. On a final note on this topic, effective leaders also need to promote the organisation's values and act as exemplars of those values; they need to 'walk the talk'; this (values) is another element of good corporate governance.

---

[20] *Management Teams – Why They Succeed or Fail*. R Meredith Belbin MA PhD (1981): Butterworth-Heinemann

CHAPTER 5

HUMAN CAPITAL MANAGEMENT

Human Capital Management (HCM) is not synonymous with HR management; it is about much more than that and should not be perceived as being an HR responsibility. Every manager in an organisation, from the chairman down, has a duty to manage the organisation's assets. In today's 'knowledge-based' economy that includes a pre-eminent duty to manage its human assets, its human capital. People are more critical today, than ever before, to an organisation's success, but they represent a very volatile asset class and are more difficult to manage and predict than any other. People are as much a liability as an asset; they undoubtedly represent an organisation's greatest value potential, but they also represent its greatest risk. In the words of Dr Michael Reddy[21] (my former chairman at HPA), "In the absence of good human capital management, an organisation can unwittingly be facilitating rather than controlling counter-productive behaviour."

---

[21] Dr Michael Reddy, Chartered Clinical and Occupational
Psychologist, Executive Chairman of Reddy Co (www.reddyco.com)

Unlike many of your organisation's assets, your human capital is an intangible asset, which makes it difficult, perhaps impossible, to accurately measure quantitatively. There have undoubtedly been enormous advances in the field of what is called human capital analytics and whilst helpful, I do not believe human capital analytics provides an accurate and comprehensive quantitative measure of an organisation's human capital. It is nonetheless possible to qualitatively assess and audit it. Human capital has been defined as, 'People at work and their collective knowledge, skills, abilities and capacity to develop and innovate'. Human capital reporting aims to provide quantitative, as well as qualitative, data on a range of measures to help identify which sort of management interventions will drive successful business performance.

The obvious question is why would I want to assess/audit an organisation's human capital? If you accept the basic premise that people do indeed potentially represent both an organisation's greatest value potential and its greatest risk there is a wide range of circumstances where such an assessment/audit is not just advisable, but essential for:

- A newly appointed chairman, or CEO, wishing to gain a rapid insight into an organisation;
- A newly appointed MD wishing to gain a rapid insight into the division(s) that he/she is taking control of;
- Directors considering an acquisition/merger, and;
- Investors (individual and institutional) considering a substantial investment in an organisation.

The list is far from comprehensive and could easily include newly appointed directors/general managers. Touching on acquisitions and mergers in particular, recent studies have shown that in over 30 per cent of mergers and acquisitions (M&A) deals the participating companies had lost value and over 35 per cent experienced a neutral impact, which means that only marginally over 30 per cent of deals delivered a positive outcome. These figures suggest there is something seriously wrong with the management of the M&A process. My own experience suggests the problem is a direct consequence of the narrow financial view of M&A strategy, led by investment bankers, CEOs and CFOs, that is still very often taken. Valuing these deals only on the basis of the numbers needed to make the deal attractive to investors, stakeholders and themselves, means that shareholders are not seeing the promised benefits. Ignoring the human capital element of an organisation is a clear example of the short-sighted and, some might say, self-serving view frequently taken by advisors, analysts, executive directors and intermediaries. I find this attitude puzzling, not least because much of the value of organisations today is represented by so-called intangible assets. The reality is that, in the long term, it is an organisation's intangible assets (especially its human capital) that add to its future worth. Assuming the numbers stack up and the lawyers are content, I suggest that it is the human capital of the proposed partner/target that should be the deciding factor, since it is well known that a major cause of M&A failures is the failure to identify and address the people issues that are usually assigned to "Things we can deal with later". In essence, what you are considering is the relative strength and sophistication of an organisation's human capital management, practice and strategy, in effect its human capital maturity. There is a range of HCM models that typically focus on how an organisation can best utilise its largest and probably greatest asset: its people. The different models that are available tend to focus on different aspects of HCM, which is understandable to a degree, as few situations in organisations are the same or remain static in the long term. Some models include a strategic management element, some focus on statistical analysis, and others on empirical studies on the use of human capital. Each one provides a different perspective on human capital (management) and the investment that an organisation can/should make into its workforce. The latter two models make heavy use of data and statistics in order to provide a mathematical understanding of this business activity.

The strategic management model is used to make the most efficient use of the resources available to an organisation, the idea being to evaluate the current status of the organisation and its individual components, identify whether those components are being utilised to best effect, and to develop and implement changes as and where necessary. When utilised appropriately, this model, which shares a number of characteristics with 'Lean Management',[22] (simply put, the core idea of Lean Management[23] is to maximise customer value while minimising waste; creating more value for customers with the same, or fewer, resources) can improve the overall performance of the organisation and move it closer to achieving its strategic aims and objectives.

Statistical analysis, at its most basic and fundamental level, looks at the investments made in your people in terms of learning and development, and compensation and benefits. This model is invariably based upon basic economics as an organisation looks for the point at which the law of diminishing returns begins to apply. A note of caution here; investing in your people can produce short-term benefits, but more often (apprenticeships, internships, talent management, et cetera) it is a long-term investment. There can be no question that the advances in what is now

---

[22] The late Peter Drucker probably encapsulated the 'spirit' of Lean when he said, "The essence of management is not techniques and procedures. The essence of management is to make knowledge productive."

[23] For more information, visit www.lean.org

generally termed human capital analytics[24] have enabled significant improvements in the qualitative/statistical analysis of an organisation's human capital. The slow, but in my view inexorable, advance of integrated reporting[25] represents another step in the right direction. Integrated reporting is a process founded on integrated thinking that results in a periodic integrated report by an organisation about value creation over time and related communications regarding aspects of value creation. An integrated report is, or should be, a *concise* communication about how an organisation's strategy, governance, performance and prospects lead to the creation of value in the short, medium and long term. Integrated reporting is needed by both organisations and their stakeholders. Organisations need a reporting environment that is conducive to understanding and articulating their strategy, which helps to drive performance internally and attract financial capital for investment. Stakeholders need to understand how the strategy being pursued creates value over time and benefits both them and the organisation's clients/customers.

Empirical models involve a more advanced form of statistical analysis and require major statistical studies to determine how different variables affect an organisation's workforce. Data gathered will be both internal and external, with external data being used to generate external, comparative, trends.

I think that all of these models have merit, but I am inclined to a more holistic approach that incorporates elements of all the models that I have outlined. One such model, with which I am familiar, developed by the late Dr Michael Reddy and his team at Human Potential Accounting, is based on five factors: Talent, Wellbeing,

---

[24] *Human Capital Analytics: How to Harness the Potential of Your Organization's Greatest Asset*, Gene Pease, Boyce Byerly & Jac Fitz-Enz (Wiley and SAS Business Series)
[25] http://www.theiirc.org

People Risk, Data and Leadership. I think that this is a good starting point and it is worth understanding what the different factors mean:

- Talent – Talent tends to be organisationally specific and is greatly influenced by the type of organisation and the nature of its work. There are some significant exceptions such as: Accountancy, Audit. Finance, General Management, HR, Legal and Marketing. Talent, as an exceptional and valuable quality or attribute, exists at every level in an organisation; and rather than being some fixed quality, a core constituent lies in its potential that it can be identified and developed.
- Wellbeing – By wellbeing, I mean the physical, emotional and psychological wellbeing of your people. Wellbeing embraces both physical and mental health and is a reciprocal responsibility of both the organisation and its people.
- People risk – People risk, more properly referred to as to human capital risk, can be sub-divided into:
  - ➢ People risks, which refers to any action of an employee that may cause a cost/harm to the organisation;
  - ➢ Organisational risks, are there any policies/practices/procedures in place that will encourage/discourage People Risks? Remuneration (Reward) is an important area here; and,
  - ➢ Location risks are generally specific to the area and include: labour supply, Government labour policy and practice, education levels, recruitment standards, and; employment practices.

An effective HCM assessment/audit will address all three arrowed points and include a detailed analysis of:

➤ Absenteeism;
➤ Unwanted staff turnover;
➤ Internal conflict;
➤ Dishonesty;
➤ Health and safety;
➤ Poor decision making;
➤ Failures in corporate governance;
➤ Knowledge management;
➤ Internal and external communication;
➤ Vision and values;, and,
➤ Board and leadership behaviours.

- Data – When I refer to 'data', I am referring to people data and how the organisation is using such data. This includes turnover and absence figures, cost of recruitment, exit interview data, and much more. The management of data is a core element of human capital management. An effective HCM assessment/audit brings together much of these data, and translates them into human capital business intelligence by interrogating, analysing, collating and associating them with aspects of business performance.
- Leadership – I have devoted an entire chapter to leadership, but in the context of HCM leadership can be defined as the ability to influence people, by means of personal characteristics and behaviours, to achieve a common goal. A leader does not have to be a manager but leadership is a facet of management and just one of the assets that a successful manager should possess. Although generally viewed positively, leadership can also be

toxic a characteristic that is sometimes evident in so-called charismatic leaders. 'Toxic' leaders tend not to engender what might be referred to as 'followership' where followers have the ability and freedom to exercise their own leadership qualities without always waiting for direct top-down delegation. 'Good' leadership invariably involves significant delegation where subordinate leaders are encouraged to exercise initiative.

I am inclined to add the further factor of culture. I accept that an organisation's culture may be primarily a symptom that is indicative of the level of human capital maturity that an organisation has achieved, but it can be an effective indicator of more deep-seated issues deriving, but not immediately apparent, from a superficial examination of the other five factors. Past experience leads me to believe that the culture of your organisation and that of a proposed partner/target can be a critical success factor in M&A activity. I also accept that these six factors are not currently capable of quantitative measurement. There is, however, a range of quantitative measures that can provide a useful indication of problems and where they exist within an organisation. Some have already been mentioned, but they include:

- Absenteeism (authorised, unauthorised, category);
- Staff engagement/satisfaction surveys;
- Staff turnover, particularly unwanted resignations, categorised by reason;
- Grievances, categorised by reason;
- Disciplinary cases, categorised by reason;
- Industrial relations disputes, and;
- Employment tribunal cases.

All of these are useful indicators, but I remain to be convinced that, whether singly or combined, they provide an accurate quantitative measure of an organisation's human capital.

CHAPTER 6

HUMAN RESOURCES MANAGEMENT

I have been involved in/with the practice of human resources management (HRM) for over 30 years. During that time it has morphed from staff management, through personnel management, to human resources management, but never – please note – people management. If you accept the premise that people are an organisation's most important asset then why not 'People Management'? I applaud the (small) number of organisations that have taken the plunge and now have a Director of People Management, rather than an HR director.

I believe that in many organisations HRM can and does serve a very useful function, providing expert advice, assistance and support to line managers. HRM is not however a 'crutch', there is a tendency among some managers to put people management issues/problems in the 'too hard to do' box and refer them straight to HR. This is really bad practice, they are your people, your team and you cannot just abrogate your responsibilities by saying, "I've referred it to HR." If you are not careful, if/when there is an issue your people will simply start going direct to HR. Do you really want HR to know that you have a problem before you do? You, the line manager, should be the 'go to' person if there is a problem. Fine, talk the issue through with HR, seek their advice, and definitely use them as a sounding board (there may be repercussions – legal and organisational – that you are not aware of), but the decision is yours; the decision is your responsibility and you are accountable for the consequences (politicians, please take note).

I tend to cringe when I see the number of SMEs with a full-time HR manager. You have a hundred people working for you, you know them all personally and you may well have recruited many/most of them. Please explain why you need an HR manager. Most, if not all, of your HR administration can be handled, very capably, by a good PA/secretary. For payroll and pensions administration (you will, at some point, fall in the scope of such delights as automatic enrolment), outsource it. I am at something of a loss to understand how HR managers in most SMEs fill their time. Why not have a part-time HR manager/director, a retained consultant, or an NED with a strong HR background?

I was talking recently to a very experienced finance director and we both agreed that what most SMEs really needed was access to affordable business expertise that was available when needed. Wishful thinking? Anything but, appoint Non-Executive Directors (NEDs) with the expertise you need; they are invariably very experienced and objective; they also tend to have multi-sector experience that enables them to bring a different perspective to bear and an extensive network of contacts. NEDs are expensive you may think, but no they are not. Typically, you might pay an NED £15,000 per annum for attending 12 board meetings, so that is £1,250 per day – shock, horror – but it does not work like that, according to my colleague Nigel Harrap of Portfolio Exec™,[26] typically an NED will devote

---

[26] http://www.portfolioexec.com/

a minimum of three days a month to her/his role, which makes the true cost less than £420 per day. Add to that the fact that you can make a telephone call, or send an email and NEDs actually represent really good value for money.

I do find it slightly strange that many organisations want NEDs with a background in the same sector. NHS Trusts demonstrate this tendency, but they are by no means unique and it isn't a tendency that is restricted to the public sector:

- NHS Trusts employ hundreds of clinicians. Their CEOs invariably have a clinical background, as do some/many of the Trusts' executive directors; so why do they insist on NEDs with a similar background? Is this a well-trodden path leading to (the dangers of) 'Group Think'?
- Financial services organisations, including banks and building societies, almost invariably want NEDs with a background in financial services. I rather thought that if the financial crisis of 2008 had taught us nothing else it was that these companies need independently minded NEDs who will not shirk from asking awkward/inconvenient questions.

HR professionals tend, I am as much at fault as anyone, to write policies, procedures and processes that can only be properly interpreted/understood by other HR professionals. Not long ago, I was working with one of the largest train operating companies in the UK. We were having a major clear out, prior to moving offices, and I found myself reading a document written some 20 years previously and realised, to my horror, that I had written the document (a grievance procedure). It was awful and I immediately shredded it. As Graham Smedley, my good friend and colleague, has pointed out to me, I should have been courageous, framed it and kept it as a reminder of the bear traps we can all fall into. Lesson learned – write your policies, procedures and processes so they can be understood and implemented by people without an HR background. The lesson for line managers and directors is quite simple, if you do not understand a proposed policy/procedure, or would not feel competent to implement it then there is something wrong with it. HR policies, procedures and processes need to be understood by everyone; those to whom they apply and those who have to apply them.

So why have all these HR (people) policies, processes and procedures? You do not have them because your HR advisor tells you that you should. You do not have them because they may give you some form of defence should you end up at an employment tribunal, albeit that is not in itself a bad reason. You have them because they are part and parcel of good people management.

Assuming they apply across your organisation, which they should, then they enable you to ensure consistency in your treatment of every single person in the organisation. Every one of your people will know that everyone is treated in the same way and that there are no 'special cases', no favouritism, and no exceptions.

Equity of treatment is important, but it is slightly disingenuous for me to say that there are never exceptions; of course there are, but they are occasions where, and only after careful consideration, you decide that there are sound business/organisational reasons for applying a different standard. Typically this situation might arise where someone in a business critical position is simply failing to perform and this is having an adverse effect on the organisation and/or the people. It may be that the individual, due to changed business circumstances, simply cannot adapt sufficiently to meet the challenges. Whatever the reason, you owe it to the individual concerned to have a discussion with her/him about the situation. In such a situation, the 'fall-back' position is invariably what is commonly referred to as a 'Compromise Agreement'. If you chose this (Compromise Agreement) route then get the Agreement drawn up by an employment lawyer.

Compromise Agreements are the 'fall-back', but they are not the only solution. At one point in my career I was exited from an organisation where I had been COO and responsible for a successful turnaround. The legal advice was a Compromise Agreement, which my then Chairman and I ignored. He and I had formed a personal relationship, founded on mutual trust and respect that continues to this day. He knew that I was passionately committed to the success of the company and would never say, or do, anything that might damage it. In such a situation a Compromise Agreement would have been counter-productive; it would have implied a lack of trust between us.

You should be aware that many/most HR professionals do not relish detail. I do not, but I am also aware that attention to detail is essential for any HR professional to be truly effective and, as a result I am quite 'anal' about detail. One of my colleagues, now group HR director of a substantial plc, was amazed when I told her that I did not enjoy detail. It is because I do not enjoy it that I work so hard at it, ensuring accuracy, brevity and clarity. Successfully restructuring organisations (large and small) involves collecting, collating and interpreting large amounts of data; there are no shortcuts! The same applies, only more so, to restructuring occupational pension arrangements where you also have to 'cleanse' the data; I have yet to come across a situation where the data held by HR, payroll and pension scheme administrators are in agreement. Never get involved in any sort of consultation (individual, or collective) unless you are absolutely certain that the data that you are working with is 100 per cent accurate.

This talk of data leads me inexorably to the issue of HR Information Systems. Such systems are not provided for the convenience of your HR people; they are provided for the benefit of the organisation and as such relevant data need to be shared, not hoarded. All too often the user specification for an HRIS tends to reflect the needs of HR, rather than those of the organisation and its people managers. HR should be the 'sponsoring' department for an HRIS, but it needs to take account of the needs of its customers, including: the board, line managers, the people and other departments. If you have, or intend to acquire, an HRIS do make sure that it is integrated with your accounts, payroll and time and attendance recording systems.

One of the problems with HR records, whether computerised, or hard copy, is ensuring that they are accurate and current. With an HRIS this problem can be greatly reduced by the introduction of 'self-service' for employees and line managers. If an employee changes address, changes their bank, gets married/divorced, then make it their responsibility to change their own personal record. If a line manager identifies a particular training need, or is concerned about an employee's attendance record, then make it their responsibility to record that fact.

Many HR professionals tend not to be particularly commercially aware, which is not necessarily their fault, but it is a fault nonetheless that they need to rectify. To make a real contribution to an organisation, HR professionals need to understand the organisation that they are working in/with and they need to have a sound understanding of financial management and the management of business.[27] Without these skills, how are you going to able to construct a robust business case for expenditure on a new HR Information System? How are you going to convince the CEO/CFO of the business benefits of learning and development activities? All too often nowadays people enter the HR profession via a first

---

[27] *Pan Management Guides, The Management of Business* (Roger Oldcorn) first published 1987

58

degree that has nothing whatsoever to do with the reality of managing an organisation. They then, often, go on to secure a Master's in an HR-related subject, which is fine if your horizons do not stretch beyond HR. If you really want to influence the organisation, you need to speak the organisation's language, which means understanding finance and commerce.

Regrettably, many organisations do have a tendency to underestimate the positive contribution that HR can make to their success. As an example, look at mergers and acquisitions (M&A). Organisations spend a lot of time and money on due diligence before proceeding with a merger, or acquisition. They spend huge sums on accountants, lawyers and many and various professional advisors, but what are they actually acquiring? In today's knowledge-based economy, what they are actually acquiring is people; their expertise, their knowledge and their talent. So how much time and money is spent on looking at the culture and people in your proposed partner/target? Invariably, the answer is not a lot and yet it is people that will make the deal work, it is people who will achieve successful integration and the economies of scale/benefits of synergy.[28] Alternatively, it is the culture and quality of the target business's management and its people and a failure to understand the implications that can be the root cause of M&A failure.

I have yet to find a single instance where as much time and effort has been expended on carrying out due diligence on an organisation's human assets (human capital) as on its financial data; I have personal experience of one that came close and, perhaps unsurprisingly, that was a company whose business is the delivery of outsourced HR and payroll services This is an area where HR could make a real difference, by carrying out a comprehensive audit of an

---

[28] An article, by the author, on this topic can be found at http://www.robertpurse.co.uk/articles-publications.cfm

organisation's human capital as part of the due diligence process. It is not something that would just benefit organisations involved in M&A activity; institutional investors and asset management companies would benefit from knowing more about the human capital of the organisation in which they were proposing to invest.

At first sight, this idea of auditing an organisation's human capital might seem to many people to be predominantly one for the private sector; this is not the case. With the amalgamation of NHS Trusts, fire and rescue services and police forces, or at the very least the amalgamation of their 'back office' services, this type of activity in the UK public sector is, I suggest, likely to grow exponentially. I am not making a political point when I say this; the new reality for all public sector organisations, certainly in the United Kingdom, is that for the foreseeable future funding is going to be very significantly constrained and in all likelihood reduced, which means that amalgamations and mergers will become more common.

Disputes/grievances will arise in even the best managed of organisations and it is good practice for organisations to have a formal (written) grievance procedure. All your people then know that if they have a grievance there is an established procedure that is intended to help to resolve such workplace conflicts. There are, however, some problems associated with in-house grievance procedures:

- The outcome of a grievance hearing invariably results in 'winners' and 'losers'. The winner will feel vindicated, but the loser will, in all probability, feel aggrieved at the outcome.
- If a grievance is lodged against a manager, or against the organisation, the individual may well be suspicious that the odds are stacked against them.

This is not an ideal situation – in the worst case, you may end up defending a claim of constructive dismissal at an employment tribunal. In the best case, you probably end up with two people who do not work well together.

A number of organisations have sought to address these problems by introducing workplace mediation/conflict resolution. Some organisations have gone so far as to make it an integral part of their grievance procedure; I am absolutely convinced that workplace mediation can deliver real and lasting benefits, but I believe that this is a step too far. I think that you can offer mediation as an addition to the formal grievance procedure, but I do not believe that you can impose mediation; for mediation to work all the parties have to be willing participants in the process. You will probably have noticed that I refer to workplace mediation as an addition to the grievance procedure, rather than an alternative. If mediation fails then the employee should retain the right to pursue a formal grievance. If mediation is available then, in the event of one of your people lodging a grievance, you should offer it and, I believe that they should take up the offer.

Some organisations have now started to use their own in-house mediators, which I consider to be generally good news. My welcome is subject to a number of caveats:

- Such people need to be fully trained by an appropriately accredited organisation, such as: ACAS,[29] John Crawley Mediation,[30] and CEDR.[31]
- They need to be of sufficient credibility and experience for their findings to be listened to.
- They need to be trusted to be both independent and objective. This point is important in all organisations, but none more so than unionised

---

[29] http://www.acas.org.uk/ciwm

[30] http://www.johncrawleymediation.co.uk/mediation-training

[31] http://www.cedr.com/skills/misemployment/

organisations. If the employee relations environment is confrontational then TU officials are likely to question the independence and objectivity of in-house mediators.

If you want to keep abreast of human resources management developments and issues, there are some excellent groups on LinkedIn.[32] Many legal firms now produce regular (free) email newsletters and updates on employment law developments and issues. They tend to be quite generic, but I find them and the accompanying analysis useful; I use two, Clarks legal[33] and Pinsent Masons,[34] but the choice is yours.

No chapter on human resources management would be complete without some mention of employee relations (ER). Establishing and maintaining positive ER with your people is a fundamental element of good people management and it involves many of the issues covered in this book. If you treat your people with consistency, dignity, fairness and respect, then you are on the right track. Effective communication is crucial, as are your behaviours, policies, procedures and values. In my experience, organisations get the ER that they deserve. If you treat your people fairly, with dignity and respect, the likelihood is that you will develop a positive employee relations environment.

If you and your organisation work to promote good ER, the likelihood is that your people will never feel the need to join a trade union or, more importantly, seek formal recognition of their trade union. You may be working in an organisation that already has recognised trade unions; the good news is that contrary to what some might say, or think, trade unions and their officers are neither luddite, nor

---

[32] https://uk.linkedin.com/

[33] http://www.clarkslegal.com/

[34] http://www.pinsentmasons.com/

are they (as a rule) deliberately obstructive; they invariably seek to act in the best interests of their members, which is precisely what their members are paying them to do. Trade union (TU) full-time officials are, in my experience, both professional and pragmatic. Over the years I have met a number of TU general secretaries and without exception they were all articulate and intelligent people. TU officials also respect matters that are discussed in confidence. In over 35 years of dealings with trade unions I have only once known a trade union official to breach a confidence.

CHAPTER 7

REPUTATION

There used to be a saying, "My word is my bond", which is perhaps in the light of recent events, somewhat ironic since it tended to be associated with the world of banking and finance. Reputation and, by implication, trust is hard won, but easily lost:

- ➤ The damage done to the reputation of the global banking industry by the financial crisis of 2008 will, I believe, take decades – perhaps a generation – to repair.
- ➤ Who can measure the reputational cost of the 'horsemeat' scandal of 2013 to amongst others, Tesco?
- ➤ What are the long-term reputational costs to Bangladesh as a country and its economy of the Rana Plaza disaster of 2013?
- ➤ What was the reputational cost to the staff of the *News of the World*, following the phone hacking scandal (2005 – 2011)?
- ➤ What was the reputational cost to MPs following the expenses scandal of 2009?

The list is pretty well endless and readers can doubtless think of their own examples in all countries and sectors. For me the key issue is that this loss of reputation was largely attributable to the actions of individuals, whether acting alone or collectively, which is part of the reason that your people are not just your greatest asset, but also, potentially, your greatest liability. Organisations, I would suggest, unless they are not concerned with their reputation, which would be worrying indeed, need a clear set of values.

An organisation's values are neither something created by the board and promulgated like the Ten Commandments, nor are they the creation of the HR Department. If you want your people to take ownership of your values, you should involve them in their formulation. The board/executive needs to show leadership and should develop the first draft for discussion; this also serves the useful purpose of showing all their people that this is something that they (The board) consider important. We are not talking *War and Peace* here, your values statement should summarise the organisation's core values in language that all your people, together with your customers and suppliers, can understand. You are probably talking about no more than a list of 8–10, so no more than a single A4 page in large type. If in doubt, apply the 'KISS' principle; keep it short and simple.

So how do you involve your people in the formulation of your organisation's values? My suggestion would be to include it as a 'big ticket' item in your regular team briefings. In larger organisations there may well be some form of employee consultation forum, if so then get it on the agenda for that body. Once you have a final draft, then you might consider circulating it to customers and suppliers for any comments. Ultimately this is about reputation and how your values will reinforce it and underpin it, so why not involve customers and suppliers in the process?

There is a major problem with having a statement of values and that is that everyone, and I do mean everyone, particularly the board, has to 'walk the talk' and their behaviours have to reflect the values. However, in due course, they will become part of the organisation's culture, 'the way we do things here'. This then has major and long lasting benefits for the organisation:

- ✓ It helps with recruitment. It enhances the organisation as an 'employer of choice'. Applicants have some understanding of the culture of the organisation, before they apply;
- ✓ New starters understand the values expected of them;
- ✓ Deviation from the values will result in peer group pressure;
- ✓ Customers and suppliers will appreciate being associated with an organisation with clear values that it adheres to; and,
- ✓ Reputational risk will be reduced.

So what might your values statement contain? I am not going to be prescriptive, every organisation must develop its own values, but here are some general thoughts to start the process moving:

Organisations such as NHS Trusts and Social Services departments, which have certainly experienced their fair share of reputational issues in recent years, can simply substitute clients and/or patients for customers. I am certain that many, perhaps most, such organisations already have a values statement, but the key issue is that they really do have to 'walk the talk'; a values statement is not simply 'window dressing'. The Mid-Staffordshire NHS Foundation Trust had a values statement, which is reproduced below. I shall not comment on the content, which I have not changed, but would ask a couple of fairly simple questions:

- Had all of the Trust's staff taken real ownership of these values and accountability for them, could the scandalous conditions have ever arisen?
- Had the Trust's board and executive 'walked the talk' and been seen as exemplars of the values, would the scandal have come about?

- We value our people and our people value our customers and suppliers.
- We treat all our people with dignity and respect and our people treat their colleagues and customers with dignity and respect.
- We act with honesty and integrity in all our business dealings.
- We actively encourage openness and honesty within our organisation.
- We encourage initiative, coupled with responsibility.
- Our reputation is critical to our success. Our people are actively encouraged to protect our reputation.
- We encourage our people to voice their concerns when they believe that colleagues are not acting in accordance with our values.

Table 3
Some Generic Values

My answer, on both counts is probably not and many people have suffered and continue to suffer as a direct consequence of that failure. One, or two, individual failures would be understandable albeit disagreeable, but the problems at 'Mid-Staffs' were endemic. The scandal concerns appalling failures in patient care and high mortality rates amongst patients at the Stafford Hospital, England, in the late 2000s. The Nursing and Midwifery Council (NMC), the UK's regulator of nurses and midwives, has held hearings about nurses working in the trust following allegations that they were not fit to practice and has struck off from their register and suspended numerous nurses as a result of these hearings. Those nurses lost their livelihoods, whereas the Trust's Chief Executive went on to become the Chief Executive of Impact Alcohol and Addition Services and the then Chief Executive of NHS West Midlands went on to run the Care Quality Commission.

It would be unfortunate and wrong if all NHS Trusts were to be tarnished by the scandal at 'Mid Staffs'. There are exemplars of superb care, kindness and excellent treatment. Based on my personal experience, here are some shining examples:

- ✓ University Hospitals Coventry and Warwickshire NHS Trust (Rugby and Walsgrave);
- ✓ Oxford University Hospitals NHS Trust (John Radcliffe);
- ✓ South Warwickshire NHS Foundation Trust (Warwick); and,
- ✓ West Midlands Ambulance Service NHS Trust.

Our Values

Together with our staff we have developed a set of Themes and Values which, along with our motto 'Because We Care' form a framework for a positive and supportive environment for our patients, visitors and staff. It is only through our staff's commitment to the care they provide that our Themes and Values can continue to be fulfilled.

Care for people

We are caring and compassionate in all that we do

We put the care and safety of our patients at the centre of the way we work

We are courteous, considerate and respectful to our patients and their families, and to our colleagues

We protect the dignity of our patients and their families, and of our colleagues

Listen and improve

We actively seek the views of our patients and communities, and respond by improving our services

We actively seek the views of our colleagues, and respond by improving the ways we work together

We believe that we must never stop learning and finding better ways of working

We help our colleagues to maintain and develop their capabilities

Work together

We work together as one team to deliver safe and caring service to our patients

We communicate and share information to deliver efficient and effective service to our patients and our colleagues

We are accountable to our colleagues for our personal contribution to the delivery of service to our patients

Do the right thing

We understand and respect the frameworks and guidelines that regulate our work

We challenge any process that stops us delivering safe, caring service to our patients

We do what we say we will do

We are open and honest

We are committed to our patients and our colleagues

There have, in recent years, been a number of cases – the horsemeat scandal being just one –where organisations have suffered significant reputational damage because of failures in their supply chain. Those same organisations very often make extensive use of audits of their suppliers. Such audits, which undoubtedly have their place, tend to rely upon the honesty of the auditors and the honesty of suppliers, neither of which can be assured. I do not doubt the honesty and integrity of most auditors and suppliers, but if a supplier is cutting corners are the auditors/you going to get honest answers? As my former colleagues at Responsible Trade Worldwide[36] (RTW) would say, one part of the answer is to "Give the People a Voice". Organisations like RTW provide that part of the answer through properly validated and anonymised surveys that can be completed:

- On paper;
- On-line; and,
- Via IVR (mobile telephone).

Reputation is, of course, not just about organisations, it is also about individuals and even nations. I spent more than 20 years as an interim executive and soon realised that, in the eyes of a potential client, I was as good as my last assignment. That meant that establishing and maintaining my (good) reputation was crucial to continued business success. Some interim service providers will say that there are thousands of interim executives in the UK, which is untrue. There are certainly thousands of independent

---

[35] http://www.midstaffs.nhs.uk/Work-For-Us/Our-Values.aspx
[36] http://www.responsibletradeworldwide.com

contractors, but perhaps only a thousand, maybe even as many as two thousand interim executives and not one of them can afford damage to their reputation; bad news travels very fast!

Reputation is also inextricably linked with corporate governance; failures in corporate governance can have a massive and negative effect on an organisation's reputation and may even imperil its very survival.

CHAPTER 8

CORPORATE GOVERNANCE

At its core, as I explain later in this chapter, corporate governance (I much prefer the expression 'good governance') is about accountability and values; this means that it is inextricably linked with the management of people. It is your people who:

- Implement the systems, policies, and processes that underpin effective/good corporate governance;
- Monitor the day-to-day operation of those same systems, policies and procedures; and,
- Accept day-to-day accountability for corporate governance in your organisation.

Corporate governance, or to be more accurate failures in corporate governance, has been much in the news in recent years. Failures at NHS Trusts and on the part of financial institutions are frequently quoted examples of such failures, but we should remember that organisations such as these, unlike Enron, FIFA and Parmalat, are subject to strict regulation by regulatory bodies such as the Care Quality Commission,[37] the Financial Conduct Authority[38]

---

[37] http://www.cqc.org.uk

and the Prudential Regulation Authority.[39] This suggests to me that whilst the organisations concerned may have failed in their corporate governance obligations, so too have the regulators. It also suggests that, in common with corporate values, you cannot simply impose effective corporate governance. You can, of course, impose the systems and processes and you can also impose legislation and regulation, but unless the principles of good corporate governance and an organisation's values are fully aligned then good governance will never become fully embedded in an organisation.

So what is corporate governance? Broadly speaking, it means the processes, relations and systems by which organisations are controlled and directed; corporate governance should not be confused with management. An organisation's governance arrangements must identify the distribution of accountability, rights and responsibilities among the different stakeholders in the organisation. These stakeholders may include, among others, the board of directors, managers, Government departments, shareholders, creditors, auditors and regulators. An organisation's governance structure should include the rules and procedures for making decisions in corporate affairs. Corporate governance includes the processes through which organisations' aims, objectives and values are set and pursued in the context of the social, regulatory and market environment in which they operate. Corporate governance processes and systems include monitoring the actions, policies and decisions of organisations and their agents, in which category I include their suppliers. Corporate governance is therefore about what the board of an organisation does and how it sets the **values** of the organisation.

---

[38] http://www.fca.org.uk

[39] http://www.bankofengland.co.uk/pra

In the UK, the generally accepted 'gold' standard on corporate governance is provided by the UK Corporate Governance Code.[40] The first version of the UK Corporate Governance Code was produced in 1992 by the Cadbury Committee and it still (Paragraph 2.5) provides the classic definition of the context of the Code:

"Corporate governance is the system by which companies are directed and controlled. Boards of directors are responsible for the governance of their companies. The shareholders' role in governance is to appoint the directors and the auditors and to satisfy themselves that an appropriate governance structure is in place. The responsibilities of the board include setting the company's strategic aims, providing the leadership to put them into effect, supervising the management of the business and reporting to shareholders on their stewardship. The board's actions are subject to laws, regulations and the shareholders in general meeting."

I have no issues with the broad principles contained in the Code, but I do have concerns regarding its limited scope and restrictive wording. The shareholders' role is limited to satisfying themselves that there is an appropriate governance structure in place. For my part, I would like to see 'effective' inserted in the wording; corporate governance structures and systems can be appropriate, but that does not of itself mean that they are effective.

If we accept the general principles set out in the Code then why should it not be more generally applicable? The Code applies principally to 'listed' companies and primarily to 'Premium' listed companies, which I think is unnecessarily restrictive. Although in 2015 there were

[40] https://www.frc.org.uk/Our-Work/Codes-Standards/Corporate-governance.aspx

around 8,350 UK registered companies with a turnover of £100M or more, there were only around 2,450 'listed' companies. Many commercial organisations, some of very considerable size, no longer seek a stock market listing and are thus, with some exceptions, not in scope of the Code. There are many other organisations with very substantial revenues that also fall outside the scope of the code.

Such organisations include:

- Charities;
- Educational institutions (academies, city technology colleges, universities, et cetera);
- Government executive agencies/trading funds;
- Local authorities; and,
- NHS Trusts.

Most of these organisations are subject to some form of regulatory framework, but many of the regulators have a remit that is largely restricted to either financial, or professional, standards. Both of these have a role to play and I am not suggesting that they can be replaced by or, in some way, subsumed into the Code; I simply believe that having a single, common, standard for corporate governance in the UK is a good idea for all organisations and their stakeholders. Corporate governance should neither be confused with professional ethics, regulation and standards, which I believe should be subordinate to a single, universal Code of Corporate Governance, nor should it be a tick-box exercise.

Do we really need the current proliferation of codes of (corporate) governance? Do charities, local authorities, NHS Trusts, schools, voluntary organisations, and the rest, really need their own (entity-specific) codes of governance? I think not; I believe that, with minor amendments, the UK

Corporate Governance Code could and should be universally adopted.

My general proposition is that all organisations with revenues in excess of £100M should be in the scope of the Code; the £100M figure is entirely arbitrary, but seems to me a sensible threshold. I have deliberately chosen revenues/turnover because of its simplicity and relative transparency. I also propose that any organisation be encouraged/permitted to voluntarily subscribe to the broad principles of the Code. I accept that such a move would involve some work on the part of the likes of the Charities Commission, Financial Conduct Authority, and Government departments, but I believe that it would be well worthwhile. In her recent book (*Good Company*)[41] Laurie Bassi stated:

"*Many companies during the past decade have launched disparate initiatives such as becoming an employer of choice, reducing carbon footprints and beefing up compliance efforts. But firms that aim to succeed in sustainable ways must move to become good companies through and through.*"

If we substitute 'organisation' for 'company', or 'firm' then I think that this paragraph becomes relevant to all manner of organisations. In the same way, we can take paragraph 2.5 of the original (Cadbury Committee) UK Corporate Governance Code (see above) and with a very few alterations, it takes on a much wider scope:

Corporate governance is the system by which organisations are directed and controlled. Boards of directors, governors and trustees are responsible for the governance of their organisations. The shareholders'/stakeholders' role in governance is to

---

[41] Bassi, L., Frauenheim, A., McMurrer, D., with Costello, L. (2011). *Good Company, Business Success in the Worthiness Era*. Published by Berrett-Koehler Publishers Inc.

appoint the directors, governors, trustees and the auditors and to satisfy themselves that an appropriate and effective governance structure is in place. The responsibilities of the directors/governors/trustees include setting the organisation's strategic aims, providing the leadership to put them into effect, supervising the management of the organisation and reporting to shareholders/stakeholders on their stewardship. The actions of the directors, governors and trustees are subject to laws, regulations and ultimately the stakeholders.

Corporate governance is inextricably linked with accountability and values. Without the clearly defined distribution of accountability, corporate governance structures and systems, no matter how well designed, are missing an essential ingredient. To use the analogy of Adair's interlinking three circles (see Leadership above), all three elements of accountability, structures and systems need to be present if an organisation is to have effective corporate governance. If any one element is missing, or incomplete then the other two elements are left incomplete.

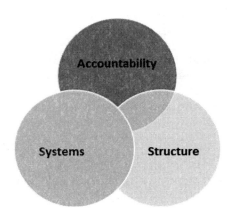

Figure 2
A Model for Corporate Governance

I firmly believe that for effective corporate governance organisations need a clear set of values and it is arguable that corporate governance must be 'values based' if it is to become fully embedded in the organisation's culture. Having a clear set of values does not necessarily mean that an organisation must have a written statement of values. In some organisations their core values are so deeply embedded that such a statement is almost superfluous. Such an organisation might be the British Army; true, there have been occasional failures, but they have invariably been isolated rather than endemic. Unless your organisation has had the benefit of more than 300 years in which to develop and embed its values, a written and publicised statement of values would seem a good idea.

Effective/good corporate governance and a clear set of values are integral to being a 'good' organisation and, as Laurie Bassi has demonstrated, being a good company/organisation is good for business. Being 'good', provided it is also accompanied by consistency and transparency, will have a number of significant benefits:

- ✓ It will enhance your organisation's reputation generally;
- ✓ It will give consumers, customers, suppliers and potential investors' confidence;
- ✓ It will help establish/enhance your reputation as 'An Employer of Choice';
- ✓ It will, to a degree, enable you to differentiate (positively) your organisation from others; and,
- ✓ It will facilitate increased engagement, loyalty and trust on the part of your people.

In my experience, there is a tendency to conjoin corporate governance with audit/compliance and risk management. I consider this inappropriate as it attempts to combine the strategic (corporate governance) with the operational (audit and risk management), which is not intended in any way to diminish the importance of the likes of audit, internal controls and risk management. They are essential elements of the framework that underpins effective corporate governance; they provide some of the checks, balances and monitoring needed to facilitate good corporate governance.

There is also a pronounced tendency in many organisations to view corporate governance and associated activities (e.g. audit and risk management) from a purely financial perspective. The financial perspective is clearly important, but if you accept the premise that people are potentially an organisation's greatest liability, I contend that, in matters of corporate governance, an organisation's people (human capital) are of equal importance to financial matters.

Although the board's role is pivotal, corporate governance is not the sole responsibility of the board. It is the responsibility of everyone employed by an organisation. There is a proverb:

For want of a nail the shoe was lost; For want of a shoe the horse was lost;
For want of a horse the battle was lost; For the failure of battle the kingdom was lost;
All for the want of a horse-shoe nail.

The proverb has been attributed to a number of people, not least William Shakespeare, but for me its importance lies in the interpretation. It describes a situation in which a failure to anticipate, or correct, some initially apparently minor problem leads progressively through increasingly critical stages to a disastrous outcome. It follows that although corporate governance and accountability are seen primarily as matters for and the responsibility of, the board and executive management, they are actually matters for and the responsibility of all employees. This cannot happen without clarity, consistency and transparency. For me, effective corporate governance is inextricably linked with an organisation's culture, its values and its people.

Effective/good corporate governance needs to be embedded in an organisation. As legislation and regulation change, so must an organisation's corporate governance systems, processes and structure. However, if an organisation's approach to corporate governance is values-based and is an integral part of its culture then such changes will be adaptive/evolutionary in nature, rather than requiring revolutionary change. This is one of the principal reasons that I prefer the UK's incremental (comply, or explain) approach to that adopted by some other jurisdictions, most notably perhaps the USA with the Sarbanes-Oxley Act 2002[42] and the Dodd-Frank Wall Street Reform and Consumer Protection Act 2010.[43]

Let us put aside, for the moment, the board and consider corporate governance at a more fundamental, but equally important, level. I accept that corporate governance is essentially strategic, but looking back at my proposed model sound/effective corporate governance needs to be underpinned by the actions of all your people, especially your people managers. Do you fully consider and take account of corporate governance and your organisation's values when undertaking for example:

- Performance reviews;
- Recruitment & Selection;
- Pay reviews?

You may be wondering what relevance these have to corporate governance, so let me provide some examples:

Performance reviews are an element of performance management, which includes learning and development,

---

[42] http://www.sec.gov/spotlight/sarbanes-oxley.htm

[43] http://www.sec.gov/spotlight/dodd-frank.shtml

and organisation design and effectiveness. The objective-setting that should be an integral part of the performance review process is not just about operational objectives, it is also about organisational objectives/values and the behaviours that underpin the successful achievement, maintenance, and promotion of those objectives and values,

When you are engaged in recruitment and selection, apart from looking for people with the appropriate experience and skill-set, you are/should be also looking for people with the right values, people who will promote and support your organisation's values and, inter alia, your organisation's approach to corporate governance, and;

Pay reviews, or more accurately, pay structures, should be focussed on promoting the long-term success of your organisation, rather than short-term benefits/gains. Structures that encourage the pursuit of short-term gain can encourage, in effect approve, inappropriate risk-taking behaviours that are inconsistent with good corporate governance.

Assuming that both your approach to corporate governance and your values are explicit and transparent then all of your people will be aware of them and will have an expectation that their managers will honour them and apply them in all matters pertaining to the management of people. The same holds true for the people that you are trying to attract through your recruitment and selection activities. There is probably a detailed reference to your corporate values on your website and there is almost certainly a reference to corporate governance on the same website. Unfortunately perhaps, there is also a vast amount of information available on the internet and if that information is not consistent with the values that your organisation espouses then you have a significant problem.

For more reading on this topic, I suggest both *Corporate Governance and Accountability*[44] and *Corporate Governance – Principles, Policies, and Practices.*[45] If the opportunity should arise, I recommend attending one, or more, of the events/meetings of the UK All Party Parliamentary Corporate Governance Group (APPCGG).[46] I have been fortunate enough to attend a number of the Group's events and they are very informative and interesting.

---

[44] Solomon J. (2013) *Corporate Governance and Accountability* (4th Edition), published by John Wiley & Sons Ltd
[45] Tricker, Bob (2012) *Corporate Governance – Principles, Policies, and Practices* (2nd Edition), published by Oxford University Press
[46] http://www.appcgg.co.uk/

CHAPTER 9

RECRUITMENT AND SELECTION

Recruitment and selection (resourcing) is about making sure that you have the right people, with the right skills, in the right place, and at the right time; it is not simply about filling vacancies. Recruitment should not be a knee-jerk reaction in response to someone leaving your organisation; before you decide to recruit do consider the following questions:

1.	What are the costs of not filling the vacancy?
2.	What value does this role add to the organisation?
3.	Do we need to keep this activity in-house, or should we consider outsourcing it?
4.	Does the role need to be office-based, could it be undertaken (in whole, or in part) remotely?
5.	Is there a better/smarter way of working that would avoid having to recruit someone?
6.	Do we already have people who could fill the role, which would provide a development opportunity? I am a firm believer in organisations developing their people, however, it may not be appropriate where you want to bring in expertise from another industry/organisation that is considered more advanced, more competitive, or more efficient,
7.	Do I need a full-time employee?
8.	Do I need a permanent employee, why not a 'temp', or an interim?
9.	Could I fill the role through using an 'intern'?

Table 5
A Recruitment Checklist

So you have decided that you need to recruit someone, how long do you expect them to stay in the same role – does three years sound realistic? Assuming that you are going to pay something approaching an average (UK) salary then, at 2015 costs, with National Insurance and pension contributions your organisation is going to be incurring at 2015 values c.£90,000 of costs, plus the costs of recruitment (advertising, agency fees, etc.). This means that you will probably be committing to a total spend of c. £100k, so it is worth getting it right.

Do not just recycle the old job description (JD), circumstances will almost certainly have changed since it was first written and the new JD should reflect those changes. The overall purpose of the role is very important and everything else contained in the JD should flow from and be consistent with that overarching statement. I like to think of this opening paragraph of a JD as the job holder's 'Mission Statement' and, as such, it should underpin your organisation's aims, objectives and values.

The 'Role and Responsibilities' paragraph can, if you are not careful, end up looking like something from *War and Peace*. I prefer to think of it in terms of measurable deliverables/outputs; what does the job-holder need to deliver to achieve success in the role? Clearly there needs to be that all-important link to your organisation's aims, objectives and values. If you focus on deliverables and outputs then you avoid being limited by current systems and processes that will inevitably change and evolve over time.

The 'Skills and Experience' paragraph is almost always a challenge and is probably best broken down into 'essential' and 'desirable'. For essential, read 'must have' and for desirable read 'nice to have'. Desirable comes into its own when differentiating between a number of candidates, all of whom meet your essential criteria. When assessing what is essential, I have found it useful to ask why particular skills, or experience, are essential for a particular role. The following list may provide some help.

Essential?

1. Must have industry/sector specific experience – Why? Does a spot-welder really need industry-specific experience? There are many trades and professions where the skills are clearly transferrable; accountancy, finance, general management, HR, IT, law and marketing are some that readily spring to mind. Arnold (Lord) Weinstock, an economist by training, not an engineer, turned GEC into a highly successful, global, multi-billion pound engineering business. More recently, Sir Richard Branson created Virgin Atlantic and I do not recall him being an airline pilot

2. Must be a member of an appropriate professional body. Fine for, amongst others, the accountancy, legal, medical and nursing professions, but is it really an essential requirement for HR and marketing roles?

3. Must be a graduate – For some positions this is clearly essential, but it is important to remember that not all degree courses require the same level of intellectual rigour as say engineering, law and medicine. If what you really want is a graduate level intellect, then why not use an appropriate objective test battery? One of the most intelligent people that I have worked with was not a graduate, but he possessed an intellect that was way beyond most of his boardroom colleagues, including me.

4. Must be IT literate – I always think that this should be qualified by some examples. Do you mean competent in applications such as: spreadsheets, databases, word-processing and the like, or are you looking for something else?

Table 6
Skills and Experience

The list could be endless; the key is to ask the question 'Is it really essential?'

Having revised the job description and before you think about filling the vacancy, you need to think about what you anticipate the general terms and conditions of employment will be. This is an area where, if you have one, your HR advisor/department can be really helpful; there may already be a template that you can use to help you. The following list should provide some help:

> Is the role planned to be:
>   o Full-time, part-time, job-share? I used to think that job-share was a very doubtful option, but I changed my mind. If you get two people who gel as a team, it works really well; covering holidays and sickness absence becomes much less of a problem,
>   o Permanent, fixed-term, temporary, or contractor,
>   o Office-based, home-based, or mobile? Do remember that if it is to be home-based the individual(s) will still need the equipment to do the job and that there is a safe working environment. Contrary to popular belief, home workers can be very productive and very often go the 'extra mile' in terms of commitment. They still need clearly defined and measurable objectives, and their performance needs to be regularly reviewed against those objectives,
> What are the 'normal' hours of work?
> What will the pay/salary be and will it be paid weekly, four-weekly, or monthly?
> Will there be a bonus scheme and/or other benefits such as: car allowance, company car, life assurance, and occupational pension scheme?
> What is the annual holiday entitlement?
> What will the notice period be (one week, four weeks, one month, three months, etc.)? There are varying schools of thought on this. My own view is that four weeks/one month should be the minimum.

This serves two purposes; it gives the job holder some security, but it also gives you the time to find a replacement. For more senior roles, three/six months is far from exceptional and you may well need up to six months to recruit a replacement and arrange their induction before the incumbent leaves.

The next steps are how you fill your vacancy. The first of these steps is advertising, more accurately nowadays, reaching your target audience. I advise against relying on 'word of mouth'; personal recommendation can be helpful, but it also means that you risk not finding your ideal candidate. If someone is personally recommended and has the appropriate skill-set and experience then put them on your longlist, but do not stop there.

You want your recruitment process to be open and honest, consistent with your organisations values, and you need/want to reach your target audience. Ten years ago the accepted route would probably have been to advertise in a newspaper, or journal/magazine. Times change and I am no longer convinced that such advertising, which was never cheap, offers good value for money. This generalisation holds true if your only focus is on recruitment. If you are also seeking to raise your organisation's profile then it may be worth considering; in this case, I would always seek advice from media/press relations experts as there may be better/more cost-effective alternatives. There is only one such organisation that I can personally recommend, JBP.[47] I have used JBP for two decades, its people are very professional, they give honest advice and their fees are, in my experience, very competitive.

So where do you advertise your vacancy? The increasing use of the internet has massively expanded the opportunities whilst, at the same time, substantially reducing the cost. There are dozens, probably hundreds, of

---

[47] www.jbp.co.uk

'job boards' where you can post your vacancy at little cost. You can refine your search by posting to specific LinkedIn groups. Some of these groups do have rules about the posting of vacancies, so it is worth checking. It may not be fashionable, but for some vacancies 'Job Centre Plus' still provides an excellent service

I think that there is still a place for recruitment consultants, including executive search consultants. It may well be that you lack the internal resources needed for the recruitment exercise that you are undertaking. The initial sift of applications for long-listing can be both time-consuming and resource-hungry, as can interviews (even if undertaken by telephone) to produce your final shortlist. Another reason for using such consultants is to preserve your organisation's anonymity. You may plan on exiting someone in a business critical role from the organisation and it is not going to be helpful if they find out that you are recruiting their replacement. If you decide to use a recruitment consultant there need to be some very clear ground rules:

- ✓ The consultancy is, in effect, representing your organisation, which means that it must comply with your values. Above all it must treat all applicants with dignity and respect;
- ✓ It must acknowledge all applications;
- ✓ It must keep all applicants regularly informed of the status of their application;
- ✓ It must provide feedback to unsuccessful candidates;
- ✓ It must check references for all shortlisted candidates, both in writing and, whenever possible, by telephone. I have found that referees tend to be far more forthcoming over the telephone than they are in writing;

- ✓ If the successful candidate leaves within three months of appointment, the consultancy must find a replacement at no cost to your organisation; and,
- ✓ It must undertake not to approach the successful candidate, for at least two years, with a view to poaching her/him.

Recruitment and selection is a project, so you should have a plan. The following table provides a basic template that you can amend/refine in accordance with your needs:

What is your budget for the entire exercise?	£
What is your budget for advertising?	£
Will you use recruitment consultants?	
How are you going to select your recruitment consultants?	
What is your budget for recruitment consultants?	£
Where will you advertise the vacancy?	Job Boards/LinkedIn/Press
When will you advertise the vacancy?	
How are applications to be made?	Email/hard copy/on-line
What form should applications be in?	Application form/CV with covering letter/et cetera
What is the closing date for applications?	
Who will carry out long-listing and when?	
How will long-listing be scored?	
Will you use telephone	

interviews as part of your short-listing?	
Who will conduct telephone interviews and when?	
How will telephone interviews be scored?	
What format will final interviews take?	Assessment centre/one-to-one/panel interview/et cetera
When and where will final interviews take place?	
Who will be involved in the final interviews?	
When will you take up references?	Before/after final interviews
When and how will you verify the applicants' right to work in the UK?	
When and how will you verify the applicants' qualifications?	
Who is arranging the induction programme?	

Table 7
Recruitment Template

When shortlisting for final interviews/selection, try to ensure that your shortlist has a minimum of three candidates, ideally –four to five. Any less and you rapidly run out of comparators. I would never advise one-to-one final interviews; this is a situation where two heads are definitely better than one.

I have mentioned Assessment Centres (ACs) a couple of times now. ACs are not suited to every recruitment project; they are resource hungry and time-consuming.

However, a properly constructed[48] and administered AC has a very high level of predictive validity, far better than either one-to-one, or panel interviews; they are fair and give a valid assessment of what someone can do, rather than just what they know. Properly constructed and managed ACs are easy to defend if subject to challenge. Successful challenges to the AC method are rare, which cannot be said for other types of assessment/selection. ACs often involve the use of psychometric assessments and tests; do ensure that these are selected, administered and interpreted by appropriately qualified people. In the UK such people should hold the British Psychological Society's Level A and Level B qualifications.

A couple of final points on the subject of resourcing; do make sure that you have an appropriate induction programme; it is a vital element of the recruitment process. An induction programme should be tailored to your organisation and the role, but you do not need to re-invent the wheel. Both ACAS[49] and the CIPD[50] provide some very useful guidance, which you can fine tune to meet your specific requirements and those of your new employee. An induction programme also needs to be aligned to your organisation's vision and values, and how the organisation operates. As an example, your organisation is a logistics business and you have a business operating system ('Lean' tools et cetera) and you expect people to adhere to the established parameters/rules/behaviours; the induction programme provides an ideal opportunity to introduce them. If there is any form of significant change underway, do explain the aims, objectives and impact as part of the programme. The induction process often involves new employees 'shadowing' a current employee. Shadowing

---

[48] If you decide to use an AC, get an expert to construct it, an AC is not a DIY project.

[49] http://www.acas.org.uk/index.aspx?articleid=4666

[50] http://www.cipd.co.uk/hrresourcefactsheets

can be very useful, but do ensure that the current employees to be involved have both the capability and the right mind-set. Do get people to sign that they have undertaken an induction programme. Yes, I know it is more administration, but it can provide invaluable legal protection if – for example – someone has an accident at work.

Do ensure that your people know that you have a new starter arriving and when, it can avoid serious embarrassment. Some years ago (25 years ago, if I am honest) I was appointed to my first HR director role. On my first day at work I arrived bright and early, only to find that the receptionist knew nothing about me. That was a bit of a worry but the real embarrassment came when I discovered that neither the 'acting' HR director, nor the HR department knew anything about my appointment; the MD had apparently forgotten to alert people to my impending arrival. Had an induction programme been prepared then it is probable that all relevant parties would have been informed/involved; it wasn't and they weren't.

CHAPTER 10

COMPENSATION AND BENEFITS

Compensation and benefits (reward) can be very complicated and fraught with problems, not least those arising from claims under the Equality Act 2010.[51] As mentioned earlier, my advice is, wherever possible, to keep your approach simple and keeping it simple aids: clarity, consistency, and equity (including fairness and affordability) of treatment. Always ensure that your approach to reward is fully aligned with:

- Your organisation's financial performance;
- The need to attract and retain the 'right' people; and,
- The need to reinforce your organisation's behaviours and values.

So what does reward include? It includes:

---

[51] https://www.gov.uk/equality-act-2010-guidance

- ✓ Basic pay;
- ✓ Job grading schemes;
- ✓ Pay structures;
- ✓ Overtime rates, if your organisation pays overtime;
- ✓ Performance-related benefits such as: bonus, employee share ownership plans, long-term incentive plans performance-related pay and recognition schemes;
- ✓ Hours of work;
- ✓ Occupational pension schemes;
- ✓ Sick pay;
- ✓ Annual holiday entitlement and holiday pay;
- ✓ Work-related expenses; and,
- ✓ Company cars/car allowances.

You may have noticed that I do not include payroll in the list. The reasoning is quite simple, payroll is about how your people get remunerated, not establishing the policies and rules governing their remuneration. Make no mistake, payroll management is complex and making sure that your people get paid correctly and on time is an essential element of good people management. The arrival of Automatic Pension Enrolment (AE) has made life even more complicated; you can get more information on AE by visiting the DWP website.[52] My own view, based on practical experience, is that, with just one exception, no organisation should run their payroll in-house; there are so many variables and changes that it is simply not worth the time and effort involved. If your organisation is multi-site, has overseas operations, or has grown through acquisition (where you may have multiple employers), the complexities increase exponentially. The exception that I

---

[52]

https://www.gov.uk/workplacepensions?gclid=CLmd3_Kjh8MCFa_Jt
AoddC8AJw

mentioned is organisations whose core business is the provision of outsourced HR and payroll services; it demonstrates confidence in their own systems and services.

When looking at payroll providers there are a number of points that I suggest you consider:

- Specify what you need/want. The list of what 'reward' includes (see above) should be of some help with this;
- Is the system fully compatible with whatever accounting system you use? This is crucial and if it isn't then do not bother; you will end up manually entering the same data to different systems, which increases the risk of errors occurring;
- Is the system fully compatible with any HR information system (HRIS) that you use? If you do not have an HRIS it is worth establishing whether the providers that you are talking to can provide HR administration services;
- Can they provide you with testimonials and reference sites to visit;
- Do they provide a 'helpline'? If not, then look elsewhere. When is the helpline available?
- Are they fully compliant with the Data Protection Act?
- Where will your organisation's data and that of your people be held? There is a lot of talk of 'cloud-based' solutions, but without being a Luddite I am not yet convinced. Cloud-based solutions can be hosted anywhere and may well be outside the jurisdiction of the UK, or EU.

Looking now at some of the elements that make up reward, basic pay is a good starting point. Basic pay is the starting point for a wide range of reward issues such as holiday pay, overtime rates, shift pay and sick pay. It also has a broader impact on your organisation's employment costs through employer's NI and occupational pension contributions. Assuming that you want to attract and retain good people, getting basic (starting) pay right is important; pitch it too low and the only people that you are likely to retain are those who lack the ability to find a job elsewhere. So how do we establish what basic pay should be? This used to be a time-consuming and expensive activity involving the tedious business of ploughing through pay surveys and hoping that the data provided were:

- ✓ Based on samples that were statistically valid;
- ✓ Up to date;
- ✓ Relevant to your organisation's activity and size;
- ✓ Took account of regional variations; and,
- ✓ The job that you were researching was a good match with the job identified in the survey(s).

For the majority of roles that has now changed. Much of the information you need can now be found via the internet and very often it is freely available. There are exceptions to this and for more specialised roles, including roles at executive level, there is still a place for pay and benefits specialists. I have used Croner,[53] Incomes Data Services (IDS)[54] and Hay Group[55] in the past and all provided excellent, albeit not cheap, services. When setting base pay rates I am inclined to go for between the lower quartile and median. Even when pay stagnates, as it has in recent years, this gives you the flexibility to make performance-related pay awards that keep pay within market rates. This is not a hard and fast rule; for someone with an exceptional (proven) track record, you can go to upper quartile and still retain some headroom for further

---

[53] http://cronersolutions.co.uk

[54] www.incomesdata.co.uk

[55] www.haygroup.com

progression. Michael Cope, a former colleague, adopts a slightly different approach where a pay range is divided into three pay 'zones':

- Bottom 30 per cent – developing;
- Middle 30 per cent – performing; and,
- Top 30 per cent – Excelling.

Job grading schemes are not essential, but they can be useful not least because they are 'gender blind' and they can provide a consistent framework for your pay structure. A word of caution here, do not try to invent your own job evaluation system. There used to be a tendency, particularly pronounced in the public sector, to do this; it was a nightmare and I hope the practice has now ceased. The job evaluation system that I have used most is that produced by the Hay Group. Before you introduce job evaluation and a job grading scheme, you will need accurate job descriptions that will need to identify, amongst other facts:

- The span of control of the post;
- The financial impact of the role (direct and indirect);
- Budgetary responsibility; and,
- The level of expertise required.

Like everything else connected with reward, your people will want to know that your proposals regarding job evaluation and grading are fair and equitable, so be open about them and give people the opportunity to ask questions. People tend to be suspicious about job evaluation schemes, in particular their validity and reliability. In my experience one of the best ways to allay these suspicions is to get your provider to make presentations to your people. In addition, do ensure that members of your job evaluation panel are properly trained. I would not advise getting your provider to carry out the job evaluations, which can get very expensive. However, it is good practice, in my experience, to get a small sample of your panel's results verified by the provider. This independent audit/verification will increase the confidence that your people have in the process and can prove quite cost-effective by reducing the number of appeals/grievances arising from the panel's findings. There are also a number of 'on-line' job evaluation tools provided by organisations that include Aon, Hay and Mercer

When considering job grading, my advice is to keep it simple and limit the number of grades. I can see little merit, or reason, for any organisation having more than 10 grades (NHS, please note). Even in the largest organisations such as the Army, I am hard-pressed to see any good reason for more than 12 grades. To avoid upsetting my former Army colleagues, I should explain that a job grade is not the same as a job title or rank.

Pay structures, like grading schemes, should be kept as simple and transparent as possible. Whether you like it, or not, people will talk about pay and, that being the case, transparency will avoid suspicion. After all, in listed companies the pay of top executives is transparent (providing you have the determination to plough through the turgid and convoluted prose of the remuneration report). I am not suggesting that everyone's pay should be in the public domain, simply that you have transparency regarding your pay structure. I think that there is a lot of merit in what is referred to as 'broad banding'; if your pay bands are too narrow it can cause problems.

Let us take the example of a high performer in an organisation with narrow pay bands of say median +/- 10 per cent. The job-holder was appointed on a median salary (at 2015 levels) of £25,000 and has had performance-based pay awards of 3 per cent per year for the last three years, so the job-holder is now on a salary of £27,318, which is just £182 below the maximum of £27,500. So what are you going to do at the next pay review, assuming continued high performance?

You might say:

- We know you have performed well again, but we can only award you 0.7 per cent because that takes you to the band maximum. You have effectively told the job holder that next year, no matter how well they perform, there will be no performance-related pay award. This is not likely to improve your staff retention figures;
- We do not have the flexibility to continue to give you performance-related pay awards, so we are going to promote you. This is where 'weasel words' like 'Senior' start to appear (senior supervisor, senior foreman, senior software developer, and senior systems analyst). This can cause all manner of problems. Unless there is a substantial change to the role, the job evaluation panel will not be amused, nor will co-workers and you may leave your organisation open to equal pay claims. If the new role is substantially different to the old one, the job-holder may not want it, which is not unheard of, and co-workers may/will wonder why they had no opportunity to apply;
- We are introducing a performance-related bonus scheme. Depending on the type of role, this may be appropriate, but unless carefully structured bonus schemes can be problematic; and,
- We have realised that our current narrow pay bands do not work for high performers like you, so we are going to introduce a new (broad-banded) salary structure.

One of the significant benefits of broad-banding is that it enables people, subject to performance, to progress without seeking promotion. There are many people who enjoy their work, do it well, but do not want promotion. One of the perceived problems is that with broad-banding salary bands can and often do overlap. I do not see that as a problem. If someone is promoted then you can have a simple policy that they go onto either the new grade minimum, or receive a 10 per cent pay increase, whichever is the greater.

I am not a great fan of paid overtime, particularly when it is guaranteed, or becomes 'institutionalised'. I worked in an organisation where the levels of overtime were sufficient to justify employing an additional 100 full and part-time staff and that is what we did. This was at a time of high unemployment and the recognised trade unions were absolutely supportive. There are some industries (e.g. agriculture and horticulture) where there are massive, seasonal variations in working time. In such situations it may well be worth looking at 'annual working time', which is sometimes referred to as annualised hours. Properly designed and implemented, annual working time can benefit your organisation and your people; it should reduce both overtime and unproductive time, whilst at the same time giving your people more predictable earnings. In connection with working time, it is worth considering how your organisation operates. If it customarily operates seven days a week, do your contracts of employment reflect that fact, or do they still refer to a 'normal' five-day working week of Monday to Friday with your organisation paying overtime for weekend working? The worst example I can think of was British Rail, which at the time (25 years ago) ran all of the UK's rail services 24/7, with the exception of Christmas Day, and everyone had a normal five-day working week of Monday to Friday. I cannot say with certainty, but I suspect that the NHS might be a suitable case for treatment. Overtime rates, if your organisation pays overtime, can vary massively. Historically, it used to be time and a half for weekdays and Saturdays, double-time for Sundays and treble time for bank/public holidays. Ask yourself the question, if your organisation pays overtime, why? Why not consider time off in lieu? It reduces your pay bill costs and helps your people achieve a better work/life balance. It also avoids problems with holiday pay calculations. As a general principle, overtime should be self-funding and in response to unforeseen circumstances.

Performance-related benefits such as: bonus, employee share ownership plans, long-term incentive plans and performance-related pay need to be carefully constructed and they should do what it says on the can and be performance-related. This means that you need a well-designed and managed performance management system and associated processes in place. Before you start linking any element of pay to performance, your performance management system needs to be accepted and trusted by your people and that will take time. In particular, your people need to trust their line managers to set achievable objectives, support delivery and provide fair feedback and ratings. I advise that you allow a minimum of two years before moving to performance-related pay. Year 1 should be seen as a 'pilot', where you identify any wrinkles:

- Does it measure what we want it to (Individual performance)?
- Does it measure it consistently?
- Are the results consistent with business unit/departmental/organisational performance?
- Do we need to revise the process?
- Do we need to provide additional training?,

An audit of the results, coupled with an anonymised employee survey can be quite helpful with the above.

Year 2 is about getting the process/system, together with any changes that you may have made, embedded in your organisation and ensuring that all your people understand that performance-related pay has to reflect organisational, as well as individual, performance. Organisational performance is not, nor should it be, restricted to commercial/private sector organisations. If a Government Department is not 'fit for purpose' then there should be no performance-related benefits for anyone, including senior civil servants, until the situation has been rectified. If a Government agency, NHS Trust, or school, has been placed in 'special measures' then how can any performance-related benefits be justified? This restriction should apply to everyone in the organisation. If a company cannot afford a 'general' pay award then that should also apply to the executive. Equally, if, as has been the case recently, the Government applies a cap to public sector pay awards that should apply to everyone (ministers included).

I will not go into the detail of bonus schemes, employee share ownership plans (ESOPs), long-term incentive plans (LTIP's), recognition schemes and the like; each needs to be tailored to the particular requirements of the organisation. That being said, they should all share two characteristics; no one should receive a performance-related benefit unless their performance is rated at least satisfactory and such schemes should be subject to regular review. Additionally, wherever possible such schemes should focus on the medium to long-term. The details of ESOPs and LTIPs will require specialised advice, but they should be written in plain English. If the documentation needs a lawyer, or accountant, to interpret it then tell your advisors to re-write it.

With the arrival of Automatic Pension Enrolment (AE), making some form of occupational pension provision is now a fact of life for the vast majority of organisations and neither you, nor your people can afford to ignore it. As life expectancy increases so does the length of time, even with increases in 'normal' pensionable age, that most of us will be reliant upon our pension income. Currently life expectancy in the UK is about 82 years, compared with about 72 years in 1970 and this upward trend shows no signs of tailing off. According to the Office for National Statistics[56] 1 in 3 children born now will live to celebrate their 100th birthday. It is an unfortunate, but inescapable, fact that the State Pension is not going to provide you, or any of your people, with a comfortable old age. It is also a fact that most people make totally inadequate pension provision.

If your organisation already has a pension scheme it will fall into one of two broad categories: Defined Benefit, or Defined Contribution (DC). Defined Benefit (DB) schemes are either Final Salary, or Career Average Revalued Earnings (CARE). Of these, Final Salary schemes are the easiest for your people to understand; however, they can be horrendously expensive for the employer, there have been cases in the recent past where scheme liabilities significantly exceeded the organisation's market capitalisation. CARE schemes are less expensive, but need more explanation. DC schemes, sometimes referred to as 'money purchase' schemes, are quite unlike DB schemes, where the sponsoring employer carries the risk and investment decisions are taken by the trustees, with the outcomes largely guaranteed. DC schemes place some of the responsibility and risk on individual members. Many organisations have more than one scheme in operation. In one organisation that I worked with there were multiple DB and DC schemes and multiple sponsoring employers.

If you have a DB scheme, I strongly advise that you consider the affordability and risk of maintaining the scheme. There are a range of options open to you including:

- Closing the scheme(s) to new members;
- Closing the scheme(s) to future accrual of benefits; and,

---

[56] www.ons.gov.uk

- Changing the scheme(s) from final salary to CARE.

None of these is simple and you will need professional advice. Do remember that you will still need to provide an occupational pension scheme for your people. If you do not already have an occupational pension scheme for your people, you will need to get one set up, almost certainly a DC scheme. There has been much written, in recent years, about DC (money purchase) schemes. They are not inherently bad; indeed there are some very good DC schemes. However, they do carry a greater risk for members as they are not guaranteed. One consequence of this is that individual members have to take some responsibility for how their pension 'pot' is invested

When establishing your scheme, keep your people informed about what is happening. They may have strong moral, or ethical, views about investment funds that you will want to be aware of as part of the process for selecting your scheme provider. Another important factor is the charges your provider is going to make. For smaller, specialised funds these can be relatively high and these charges come out of the pension 'pot'. When the time comes to talk to your people about available investment choices do not even think about doing it yourself, find a reputable independent financial advisor and get them to run some generic investment clinics. Everyone's financial needs differ, so there is no 'one-size-fits-all' solution to investment decisions. What your organisation might consider doing is reimbursing the cost of the first, individual, consultation with an IFA.

If you have, or are introducing, an occupational scheme it is well worthwhile considering a 'salary sacrifice' arrangement. It can be a very tax efficient way for your people to make pension contributions and it can also benefit your organisation. In brief, the employee sacrifices a proportion of their salary, which your organisation, the employer, pays into the employee's pension in addition to any pension contributions already being made by the organisation. The employee benefits from reduced Income Tax liability and National Insurance contributions (NICs) and the employer benefit from a reduction in NICs. If an employee opts for salary sacrifice, your organisation needs to consider a number of policy issues, including:

- Do we pay part of our NIC saving into the employee's pension and, if so, how much; and,
- Do we retain a notional salary for calculating such items as;
  o Pay awards;
  o Bonus;
  o Life insurance cover (if your organisation provides it).

Salary sacrifice arrangements are not suitable for everyone, but the Pensions Advisory Service (www.pensionsadvisoryservice.org.uk) provides some useful guidance for both employees and employers.

Work-related expenses should be just that, they should be expenses that are reasonably and necessarily incurred in connection with work and like all employment policies, your policy on expenses should be simple and transparent. As Albert Einstein[57] said, "*Everything should be made as simple as possible, but not one bit simpler.*" I would not expect an organisation's people to incur significant costs on behalf of their employer and then wait several weeks for that expenditure to be reimbursed. The 'normal' routine is to submit expense claims at the end of the month and get reimbursed in the next salary payment. For many routine expenses this approach is no longer appropriate, or cost effective:

---

[57] Albert Einstein (1879 –1955)

- Accommodation – Hotel bookings are invariably cheaper through an agency and your organisation retains control. You pay for a standard room, evening meal and breakfast. If the employee incurs extras then it is at their cost;
- Fuel – Fuel cards can be useful, but a 'company' credit card may be of more use. It is not restricted to particular fuel stations and can also be used for other, business-related, incidental expenses; and,
- Travel – Air and rail travel can be easily and, generally, cost-effectively arranged through an agency.

These arrangements give you traceability and they are easily audited.

Company cars can be an expensive nightmare. Everyone has different needs. So the range is never right, particularly, in my experience, for the male of the species. Some people will want to trade up and others will want to trade down, others will want diesel, or LPG; my advice is to steer well clear of providing company cars, even through leasing arrangements, and just pay a car allowance. You will need to ensure that your terms and conditions of employment clearly establish what the 'ground rules' are:

- The vehicle needs to be properly maintained, at the driver's expense, in a roadworthy condition. I would reserve the right to inspect the vehicle's maintenance records;
- It needs to be properly taxed and insured, including for businesses purposes, and I would want sight of a current certificate of motor insurance at least annually;
- The driver needs to hold a valid driving licence, which should be checked at least annually;

- The driver should be required to advise you, at the earliest opportunity, if their driving licence is endorsed. (You really do not want a driver, who has been disqualified driving around in a company-funded vehicle.); and,
- The allowance is conditional upon the employee being employed in a 'qualifying' grade, or job. If they cease to be employed in such a role then the allowance ceases. You might be surprised at how often organisations miss this and carry on paying car allowance, or providing a company car long after the individual ceased to qualify.

There are always exceptions and I can immediately think of one particular exception (I am sure that there are others) to my advice. Some years ago I worked with a large, multi-site, company with more than 50,000 UK-based employees. The then COO was, quite legitimately, driving in excess of 70,000 business miles a year. Nothing particularly exceptional about that perhaps, but this was someone on a salary of c. £300k per year so let us make a few assumptions:

- 70,000 miles at an average of 40 miles per hour equates to 1,750 hours of unproductive time a year. You cannot prepare for meetings whilst driving, you cannot – safely – send emails, or texts whilst driving, and you cannot – safely – read emails and texts whilst driving;
- 1,750 hours (assuming a 15-hour day) equates to c.117 days per year; and,
- You are, in effect, paying a COO to do nothing productive for 50 per cent of their working time.

Allowing for other employment costs (car allowance, ERNIC, pension contributions, et cetera) your organisation is wasting about £200k per year! Contrary to popular opinion, Government ministers are not provided with a car and driver as a 'perk', they are provided with it so they can maintain constant contact (including via email and text) and keep on working. Food for thought perhaps?

FURTHER READING

Management Teams – Why They Succeed or Fail, R. Meredith Belbin MA PhD, ISBN 0-7506-0253-8

The Handbook of Psychological Testing, Paul Kline, ISBN 0-415-05480-X

Beyond the Call, Marc Woods and Steve Coomber, ISBN 978-1-119-96258-8

Good Company – Business Success in the Worthiness Era, Laurie Bassi et al., ISBN 978-1-60994-061-4

Playing to Win – How Strategy Really Works, A.G. Lafley and Roger L. Martin, ISBN 978-1-4221-8739-5

Managing for the Future, Peter F. Drucker, published 1992, CN 3194

Corporate Governance – Principles, Policies, and Practices (2nd Ed.), Bob Tricker, ISBN 978-0-19-950796-9

Corporate Governance and Accountability (4th Ed.), Jill Solomon, ISBN 978-1-1184-4910-3

The Management of Business, Roger Oldcorn, ISBN 0-330-29776-7

Nuts, Kevin L. Freiberg and Jacquelyn A. Freiberg, ISBN 1-58799-119-5

Accounting and Finance for Non-Specialists (6th Ed.), Peter Atrill and Eddie McLaney, ISBN 978=0-273-71694-5

Working With Emotional Intelligence, Daniel Goleman, ISBN 0-7475-3984-7

Handbook of Personality Psychology, edited by Robert Hogan, John Johnson and Stephen Briggs, ISBN 0-12-134645-5

The New Generation of Human Capital Analytics, ACCENTURE. (2010). Available at: http://www.accenture.com/us-en/Pages/insight-new-generation-human-capital-analytics-summary.asp

Human Capital Analytics: how to harness the potential of your organisation's greatest asset, B. Byerly, J. Fitz-Enz and G. Pease, ISBN 978-1-118-46676-6
The Fish Rots From The Head, Bob Garratt (1996). ISBN 0-00-255613-8

INDEX